Along the Garden Path

Along the Garden Path

with Bill and Sylvia Varney

fredericksburg herb farm

First Edition
First Printing, November 1995
20,000

Copyright© 1995
Bill and Sylvia Varney/Fredericksburg Herb Farm
P.O. Drawer 927
Fredericksburg, Texas 78624-0927
(210) 997-8615

Library of Congress Number: 95-83160
ISBN: 0-9649691-0-6

All rights reserved. No part of this book may be
reproduced or transmitted in any form or by
any means, electronic or mechanical, including
photocopying, recording, or by any information
storage and retrieval system without prior written
permission from Fredericksburg Herb Farm.

Manufactured in the United States of America by
Favorite Recipes® Press
2451 Atrium Way
Nashville, Tennessee 37214
1-800-798-1780

Book and jacket design by Starletta Polster

Additional copies of *Along the Garden Path*
may be obtained from
Fredericksburg Herb Farm
(210) 997-8615

For my grandmother,
Clara Gibbs Rusk,
who always said,
"Take your time going,
but hurry back."

Contents

Preface

William Varney's gift for and love of growing plants took root early. On his eighth birthday, he received a greenhouse, obtained a tax number, and started "Bill's Greenhouse," his own nursery. Twenty-eight years later, his energy and talents have produced even more tangible results — Fredericksburg Herb Farm, a twelve-plus acre farm in Fredericksburg, Texas, with a large processing facility for the Farm's harvest, a commercial greenhouse, the Herb Haus Bed and Breakfast, and a restored historic Texas home. Built in the form of a traditional German farmhouse, the home now contains the Farm's retail shop and tea room.

Excitement at Fredericksburg Herb Farm increased when Bill's wife, Sylvia, began writing a weekly series of articles called "Making Scents of Herbs" for their local newspaper. Bill and Sylvia now write "Farm Family," their own newsletter, and "The Best of Our Harvest," their mail order catalog.

A quiet herbal Eden, the Farm changes the lifestyles of those who discover it. It is a place to stop, smell, touch, taste, and watch nature's harmony at work. It is Along the Garden Path that Farm visitors are inspired to garden, cook, bathe, and scent their homes with herbs, nature's most useful plants.

Introduction

All over the world, people have dug, dried, sniffed, chewed, pounded, rubbed, and brewed the plants around them. They searched nature for a sense of well-being. This search for "all-natural" improvement continues today; the last century has seen a dramatic growth in therapies designed to enhance emotional and spiritual well-being by making the body healthier.

To look for an herb that will flavor a tea, answer a medical need, or simply imbue your house with fragrance is a real kick. To find a flower that intrigues, enlightens, or beguiles you is an experience. Indeed, we believe that inside every person there is an herbalist waiting to be discovered. Time passes ever so quickly when working or browsing in a garden.

But no matter how long or how short the time that we've been gardening or cooking, we all need inspiration occasionally. We hope you'll find it here in a walk *Along the Garden Path*.

The Ichthus Garden

"Show me your garden and I shall tell you what you are."
— Alfred Austin (1835–1913)

A Garden Committed to Faith

A limestone-shaped Ichthus Garden skirts the entrance to Fredericksburg Herb Farm and the Herb Haus Bed and Breakfast. The ichthus was frequently used as a symbol of faith by the early Christians and thus conveys an ancient message: the initial letters of Jesus Christ, God's Son, Saviour spelled out the Greek word for "fish." Composed of seasonally colorful, symbolic biblical herbs, the Ichthus Garden serves as a gift of faith and love from those who established it to those who visit.

Won't you join us for a stroll through this Ichthus Garden chapter? It's filled with wonderful bed and breakfast-y things — teas, jams, and breads; flavored butters and spreads; a look at massage and aromatherapy; and hints for a good night's sleep.

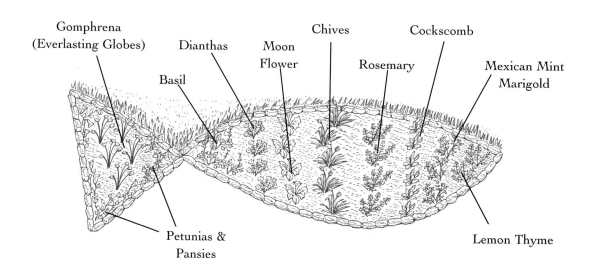

Gomphrena (Everlasting Globes) · Dianthas · Basil · Moon Flower · Chives · Rosemary · Cockscomb · Mexican Mint Marigold · Lemon Thyme · Petunias & Pansies

If you are cold, tea will warm you—If you are heated, it will cool you—
If you are depressed, it will cheer you—If you are excited, it will calm you.
—William Gladstone

Tea—the Herbal Alternative

Some like it hot, some like it cold, some like it with sugar, lemon, honey, milk, or stronger stuff, and some like it straight. But just what is tea—a beverage made only from the leaves of the *Camellia sinensis,* or any drink made from steeping fragrant leaves, berries, seeds, flowers, roots, or bark in boiling water? Or is the perfect cup one of those "heated issues" you've never considered? The French might say beverages made from herbs are tisanes, while the English might call them infusions.

That still doesn't explain people's "loyal-tea"—it's drunk more than any other liquid except water. Indeed, early civilizations brewed herbaceous plants, full of tastes and aromas, and used them to sustain life, enhance sleep, restore health, ease conversation, and as a favorite companion to food. Our take on the issue, though, is that tea is food itself! Herbal infusions, hot or cold, have become desirable caffeine-free alternatives to coffee and cocoa. In fact, several herbs (mate, guarana, cola nuts, ephedra, and gotu kola) contain caffeine or other stimulants. Herbal brews, drunk in quantity, may produce welcome or unwelcome sedative, laxative, and diuretic effects.

That said, though, experimenting—one herb tea a little at a time—is still the best way to appreciate the flavor and effect of herbs. To prepare a delicious cup, boil the water, infuse the herbs, and drink the infusion. To prepare a truly exceptional cup, use fresh cold water and full-leaf or freshly cut herbs; avoid stainless steel tea balls. For hot tea, use one bag or one well-rounded teaspoon of dried herb per cup; for iced tea, use two teaspoons per cup. Steep for three to five minutes—some blends are naturally stronger than others, so let your taste be your guide. Remove the herbs and drink up.

"Thank God for tea! What would the world do without tea?
How did it exist? I am glad I was not born before tea."
—Sydney Smith, 1771-1845

Apple Pick-Up

2 tablespoons Fredericksburg
   Gentle Wake-Up Herb Tea
2 cups freshly boiled water
3 cups chilled unsweetened
   apple juice
2 cups chilled ginger ale

Place tea in warmed teapot. Pour in water; cover. Steep for 12 minutes. Strain tea, pressing with back of spoon to extract all possible liquid; cool. Pour tea into 3-quart pitcher. Stir in apple juice and ginger ale. Pour into ice-filled glasses.

Yields 6 servings

In many parts of the tea-drinking world, tea is more than a thirst-quencher. In Burma, the tea leaf (called the "Leaf of the Gods") is pickled by mixing fruit with it and then fermenting. Add oil, powdered dried shrimp, fried garlic, nuts, coconut slices, and peas. The result? Not only dinner, but an ingredient of social custom: engaged couples are considered married once they've eaten pickled tea from the same dish. Even early Americans were unsure about tea. After receiving a gift of tea, an eighteenth century pioneer family poured boiling water on it, steeped it, and dined on it as a vegetable.

Fruit and Spice Herb Tea

Bright blue borage blossoms frozen in ice cubes are a pretty touch for iced herb teas and other summer drinks.

2 cups dried lemon verbena leaves
1 cup dried chamomile
1 cup dried orange zest
3 tablespoons whole cloves, crushed
1 (6-inch) cinnamon stick,
   crushed

Combine all ingredients in bowl; mix well. Store in tightly covered tin. When ready to prepare tea, shake tin well. Spoon 1 teaspoon tea mix for each cup of water into teapot. Pour boiling water over tea. Steep for 5 to 10 minutes.

Yields 4 cups tea mix

Perhaps you're inclined, as I once was, to think of drinking herb tea as something medicinal, not something to be enjoyed. What a delight to find that many herb teas are not only fragrant, but delicious—good for you and for your state of mind. To be sure, teatime is meant for herb gardeners and for their fortunate friends! To make a pot, I suggest using one tablespoon dried herb or two packed tablespoons fresh herb for each cup, plus an extra two table-spoons fresh or one dry "for the pot." For iced tea, use three table-spoons fresh or two tablespoons dried, plus extra for the pot.

"There is a great deal of poetry and fine sentiment in a chest of teas."
—Ralph Waldo Emerson

(This is more than the usually suggested "one teaspoon dried." For me, using too little of an herb produces a weak, only faintly flavored water.)

Bring fresh cool water to a rolling boil. Rinse the teapot (don't use a metal one) with some of the hot water to warm it. Then add herb leaves and flowers. Pour boiling water over the herbs, and let the tea steep for at least five minutes!

Pour out a little tea to taste until the tea is the desired strength. Remember that most herb teas are meant to be a golden-green brew; steeping them too long may produce a bitter or grassy taste. (If the tea is too weak, I add more herbs, but don't increase the steeping time.) Strain the leaves as you pour each cup. Serve with sugar, honey, rock candy, or fresh lemon or orange slices (I don't recommend milk). A splash of brandy, rum, or homemade wine for extra flavor is nice in the evening, too.

Would I go to this much time or trouble on a hot day? Not hardly! On any sunny day, sun-brewed tea is best. Please try this fresh herb blend. (Measurements are packed ones.)

1   cup fresh peppermint leaves (uplifting, wonderful for the weary)
1   cup lemon balm leaves (symbols of sympathy, said to chase away melancholy)
1   tablespoon rosemary tops (reputed to restore the memory)
3   sage leaves (symbol of domestic virtue, said to make you wise)

Place all herbs in a 1/2-gallon glass jar. Fill with fresh water. Place in full sun, moving the jar as the light shifts; shake or stir occasionally.

At the end of a long, hard day, strain the tea, add honey, and enjoy warm from the sun or iced. May a glass lead you to a sunset with quiet peaceful thoughts!

Rose Tea

Rose hips have an amazing supply of vitamin C you don't want to boil away, so be careful to simmer, not boil, the tea.

1   cup water
1   teaspoon crushed rose hips

Bring water almost to a boil. Add rose hips. Simmer for 10 minutes. Serve with honey and/or fresh lemon. If rose hips are not available, simmer 1/4 cup fresh petals in 1 cup water for 10 minutes.

Yields 1 cup

Spice-Scented Hot Chocolate

When the use of chocolate became common in the eighteenth century, chocolaterias opened in Madrid, serving hot chocolate to weary voyagers. A yummy drink to welcome your family home today!

2   cups milk
4   ounces bittersweet or
       semisweet chocolate
1   tablespoon (heaping)
       Fredericksburg Spiced
       Toddy Mix
1/2 teaspoon instant espresso powder

Combine all ingredients in heavy saucepan. Cook over low heat until chocolate melts, stirring constantly; increase heat. Bring just to a boil, stirring frequently; remove from heat. Whisk until frothy. Return to heat. Bring just to a boil; remove from heat. Whisk until frothy.

Repeat heating and whisking once more for a richer texture. Filter mixture. Pour into mugs.

Yields 2 cups

Minted Strawberry Shake

1   cup plain yogurt
1   medium banana, peeled
3/4 cup fresh strawberries
1   tablespoon wheat germ cereal
2   teaspoons honey
1   tablespoon minced fresh mint
6   ice cubes

Combine all ingredients in blender container. Process, turning machine on and off, for 5 to 10 seconds or until mixture is smooth and frothy. Pour into tall glass and slurp!

Yields 1 serving

Herb Honey

A term of endearment, a description of one's most beloved, sweet golden honey has been a favorite food—"nectar of the gods"—ever since some ancient cave-human pulled a sticky hand out of a beehive and took a lick.

~ Make a delicious fruit dip by adding 2 1/2 tablespoons of herb honey to a cup of sour cream or yogurt.

~ For a sensational toast topper or chicken glaze, blend 1/2 cup herb honey with 1 cup softened butter.

~ Replace white sugar with honey in any recipe: Use only one-third to one-half as much herb honey as is called for in sugar. Do reduce the other liquids in the recipe by up to one-fourth to compensate for the honey's liquidity.

🐝 When substituting herb honey in baked goods, add extra flour instead of reducing the liquids.

🐝 Bee-ware! Honey-baked goods brown faster than those made with sugar, so reduce the oven temperature by about twenty-five degrees.

With honeys, as with fine wines, the development of the palate is an adventure!

Rosemary Apple Jelly

We use filtered, clear apple juice for a pretty jelly. You may want to substitute 2 cups clear cranberry juice for 2 cups of the apple juice for a more tart jelly.

4   cups apple juice
3   (4-inch) sprigs of rosemary
2   ounces powdered pectin
3   cups sugar
4   (2-inch) sprigs of rosemary

Combine apple juice and 3 rosemary sprigs in large stainless steel or enameled saucepan. Bring to a boil; remove from heat. Let stand, covered, for 1 hour. Remove and discard rosemary sprigs. Stir in pectin. Bring to a boil. Boil for 1 minute, stirring constantly. Add sugar all at once; mix well. Bring to a boil that cannot be stirred down. Boil for 1 minute. Remove from heat; skim froth. Place 2-inch rosemary sprig in each of 4 hot sterilized canning jars. Pour in cooked mixture, leaving 1/2-inch headspace. Wipe rims of jars. Seal with 2-inch lids.

Yields 4 half pints

Bing Cherry Jam

4   cups chopped pitted Bing cherries
1   envelope pectin
$1/4$ cup lemon juice
$1/4$ teaspoon salt
$1/2$ teaspoon ground cinnamon
$1/2$ teaspoon ground cloves
$1/4$ cup almond liqueur or
        1 teaspoon almond extract
$4^1/2$ cups sugar

Combine cherries, pectin, lemon juice, salt, cinnamon, cloves and liqueur in large saucepan. Bring to a full rolling boil. Stir in sugar. Boil for 2 minutes; remove from heat and skim. Ladle into hot sterilized 1-pint jelly jars, leaving 1/4-inch headspace; seal with 2-piece lids. Process in boiling water bath for 10 minutes.

Yields 7 1/2 pints

How doth the little busy bee,

Improve each shining hour,

And gather honey all the day,

From every opening flower!

—Isaac Watts

Gingered Jam

1 (1-pound) can whole
     cranberry sauce
1 cup finely chopped mission figs
1 cup pineapple juice
3/4 cup packed light brown sugar
1/4 cup finely chopped
     crystallized ginger
1 teaspoon grated lemon zest
1/2 teaspoon pumpkin pie spice

Combine all ingredients in large saucepan; mix well. Bring to a boil; reduce heat. Simmer for 30 minutes or until mixture is reduced by almost half, stirring frequently. Cool to room temperature.
Pour into 1/2-pint jars; seal with 2-piece lids. Store in refrigerator.

Yields 2 half pints

Lemon Verbena Sweet Biscuits

1 (6-inch) sprig of lemon verbena
1/4 cup sugar
2 cups flour
     Grated zest of 1 lemon
1 tablespoon baking powder
1/2 teaspoon salt
1/2 cup cold unsalted butter, grated
1 egg, beaten
1/4 to 1/2 cup half-and-half
     Melted butter
     Sugar to taste

Mince lemon verbena with sugar in food processor. Combine sugar mixture, flour, lemon zest, baking powder and salt in large bowl; mix well. Stir in grated butter until crumbly. Add egg and enough half-and-half to create dough; mix well. Turn out onto lightly floured surface. Knead until smooth. Roll 1/2 inch thick. Cut with floured biscuit cutter or cookie cutter. Place on baking sheet. Bake at 425 degrees for 15 minutes. Remove from oven. Brush hot biscuits lightly with melted butter; sprinkle with sugar.

Yields 12 biscuits

Bay Hot Cross Buns

8   cups (about) unbleached flour
2/3   cup currants
2   cups warm water
7   teaspoons active dry yeast
1/2   cup warm water
1   cup milk
3   fresh bay leaves
1/4   cup light honey
2   large eggs, slightly beaten
1   teaspoon salt
1/2   cup water
1/2   cup melted unsalted butter
1   egg white

Sift flour into large bowl. Soak currants in 2 cups warm water for 15 minutes; drain and squeeze excess water from currants.

Dissolve yeast in 1/2 cup warm water. Let stand until yeast is active. Scald milk in saucepan with bay leaves; remove from heat. Dissolve honey in milk mixture. Add eggs, salt and 1/2 cup water to honey mixture; mix well. Add active yeast, honey mixture, melted butter and currants to flour. Stir with wooden spoon to incorporate approximately half the flour. Remove dough to smooth surface; knead in remaining flour. Knead for 10 minutes longer; dough should be smooth and soft but not sticky. Place dough in lightly buttered bowl. Let stand, covered with tea towel, for 1 hour or until dough doubles in bulk. Punch dough down; divide into halves. Roll each portion into long cylinder 3 inches in diameter. Cut cylinders into 1-inch slices. Roll each slice into a ball. Place on lightly buttered baking sheets. Let rise for 10 minutes in warm place. Slash top of each ball in cross shape. Beat egg white until frothy. Brush over each ball. Bake at 375 degrees for 15 to 20 minutes or until rich golden brown. Cool to room temperature. Drizzle with Simple Icing along slash marks if desired.

Yields 3 dozen buns

Simple Icing

1   tablespoon lemon juice
1   tablespoon water
1   cup confectioners' sugar

Combine all ingredients in small bowl; whisk until smooth.

Yields 1/2 cup

Scented Geranium Pesto Breakfast Buns

The aroma while these buns bake is absolutely tantalizing!

1   package fast-rising yeast
^{1}/$_4$ cup lukewarm water
^{1}/$_2$ cup sugar
2   eggs, at room temperature
1   teaspoon salt
1   tablespoon shortening
1   cup lukewarm water
1   cup milk, at room temperature
5^1/$_2$ to 6 cups unbleached flour

Dissolve yeast in 1/4 cup water in bowl; stir in sugar. Beat eggs with salt; stir into sugar mixture. Melt shortening in remaining 1 cup water and milk in saucepan. Cool to lukewarm. Stir into yeast mixture. Add flour 1/2 cup at a time, beating well after each addition; dough will be very sticky. Place dough in large well-buttered bowl, turning dough to coat surface; cover with plastic. Let stand in very warm place for 25 to 35 minutes or until dough doubles in bulk. Knead gently on floured surface; divide into 4 portions. Roll into small rectangles. Spread with Pesto Filling. Roll up as for jelly roll. Cut rolls into 1-inch slices. Place cut side down in well-buttered muffin cups. Dust with Scented Geranium Sugar (page 25). Let rise for 15 to 20 minutes or until doubled in bulk. Bake at 400 degrees for 12 to 15 minutes. Serve warm.

Yields 3 dozen rolls

Pesto Filling

Use your favorite scented geranium leaves in this filling—rose, lemon, lime, nutmeg, ginger, peppermint.

1^1/$_2$ cups sugar
^{3}/$_4$ cup unsalted butter
18   medium scented
      geranium leaves, minced
      Peels from 3 medium oranges
^{1}/$_4$ cup chopped pecans

Combine all ingredients in food processor container. Process by turning machine off and on until paste forms.

Yields 2 cups

Herb and Wine Muffins

1   cup baking mix
1   tablespoon sugar
1/4 cup chopped green onions
1   teaspoon fresh dill
1   teaspoon fresh basil
1   teaspoon fresh oregano
1   egg
1/2 cup milk
4   ounces Cheddar cheese, shredded
1/4 cup butter, softened
1/4 cup Edelblume wine

Combine baking mix, sugar, green onions and herbs in bowl; mix well. Beat egg slightly with milk in small bowl. Add milk mixture, 2/3 of the cheese, butter and wine to flour mixture; beat until blended. Spoon into well-greased muffin cups. Sprinkle with remaining cheese. Bake at 400 degrees for 15 minutes or until brown and crusty. Serve with butter.

Yields 1 dozen muffins

Herbed Pepper Muffins

1 1/2 cups flour
2   tablespoons sugar
2   teaspoons baking powder
3/4 teaspoon salt
1/2 teaspoon baking soda
1 1/2 teaspoons minced fresh basil
1   teaspoon minced fresh tarragon
1/2 cup unsalted butter
1/3 cup chopped green onions
1/3 cup finely chopped
        red bell pepper
1/4 cup finely chopped
        green bell pepper
2/3 cup sour cream
2   eggs, beaten

Mix flour, sugar, baking powder, salt, baking soda, basil and tarragon in bowl. Melt butter in heavy 10-inch skillet over medium heat. Add green onions and peppers. Cook until tender. Let stand to cool. Whisk sour cream with eggs. Stir into green onion mixture. Add to flour mixture, stirring just until blended. Fill greased muffin cups 3/4 full. Bake at 400 degrees for 20 to 25 minutes or until browned.

Yields 10 to 12 muffins

Poppy Seed and Carrot Muffins

1	cup flour
1/4	cup packed dark brown sugar
1 1/2	teaspoons baking powder
1/4	teaspoon salt
1/2	cup grated carrot
	Grated zest of 1 orange
2	tablespoons poppy seeds
1	egg, beaten
2	tablespoons melted unsalted butter
1/2	cup milk
1/4	cup golden raisins
1/4	cup walnut pieces

Combine flour, brown sugar, baking powder and salt in large bowl; mix well. Stir in carrot, orange zest and poppy seeds. Add egg, butter and milk; mix gently.

Stir in raisins and walnuts. Spoon into 6 medium or 4 Texas-size muffin cups sprayed with baking spray. Bake at 375 degrees for 25 minutes or until muffins have risen and are golden brown.

Yields 4 to 6 muffins

Rosemary Bran Breakfast Muffins

14	tablespoons unbleached flour
1 1/2	teaspoons baking soda
1	teaspoon baking powder
1/8	teaspoon salt, or to taste
1/4	cup safflower oil
1/2	cup packed dark brown sugar
1	egg, beaten
2/3	cup buttermilk
1/3	cup wheat germ cereal
1/2	cup oat bran
1	teaspoon minced fresh rosemary
	Grated zest of 1 orange
1/3	cup chopped pecans
1/3	cup chopped prunes

Sift flour, baking soda, baking powder and salt in bowl. Combine safflower oil, brown sugar, egg, buttermilk, wheat germ, oat bran, rosemary and orange zest in large bowl; mix well. Stir in pecans and prunes. Add flour mixture to buttermilk mixture; do not overmix. Chill, covered, for 1 hour to overnight. Spoon batter into greased or paper-lined muffin cups. Bake at 400 degrees for 20 minutes or until wooden pick comes out clean.

Yields 6 muffins

Soda Muffins with Cheddar and Chives

This recipe makes a big basketful of muffins, plus enough for breakfast!

4   cups flour
2   teaspoons baking powder
1 1/2 teaspoons salt
1   teaspoon baking soda
1/4   cup cold butter, cut into pieces
6   ounces sharp
        Cheddar cheese, shredded
1/4   cup snipped fresh chives
2   cups buttermilk
1   egg, beaten

Sift flour, baking powder, salt and baking soda in bowl. Cut in butter until crumbly. Stir in cheese and chives. Mix buttermilk with egg. Add to flour mixture, stirring just until blended; batter will be thick. Spoon into greased muffin cups.

Herb Flour

Create your own flour mixture by combining four cups flour with one-fourth cup mixed dried herbs of your choice.

Store in an airtight container.

Use to coat chicken or fish or use in your favorite biscuit recipe.

Bake at 350 degrees for 30 minutes or until golden brown. Serve warm.

Yields 24 muffins

Scented Geranium Sugar

Use your favorite scented geranium leaves for this sugar; it can be used to cook up the most delightfully flavored dishes.

10   to 12 scented geranium leaves
1/2   pound sugar

Gently wash leaves; pat dry. Scatter leaves throughout sugar. Let stand in tightly covered container for several days.

Yields 1/2 pound

Harvest Herb Tea Bread

Pictured on page 42.

$1^2/3$ cups flour
$2^1/2$ teaspoons baking powder
1   tablespoon grated lemon zest
$1/2$ cup pecan pieces
$1/2$ cup milk
5   tea bags Fredericksburg
       Harvest Herb Tea
$1/2$ cup unsalted butter, softened
1   cup sugar
3   eggs, beaten

Mix flour, baking powder, lemon zest and pecans in small bowl; set aside. Heat milk in small saucepan over low heat until small bubbles form around edge, stirring occasionally; do not boil. Remove from heat and submerge tea bags in milk. Let stand to cool. Squeeze excess milk from tea bags; remove and discard tea bags. Cream butter with sugar in mixer bowl until light and fluffy. Add eggs; beat well. Add flour mixture and milk mixture alternately to creamed mixture, beating well after each addition. Pour into greased and floured 4x8-inch loaf pan. Bake at 350 degrees for 35 to 45 minutes or until browned. Cool before serving.

Yields 1 loaf

No one who has ever tasted a loaf of herb bread fresh and warm from the oven could disagree with this old Spanish proverb:

"All sorrows are less with bread."

Bread Machine Poppy Seed Lemon Bread

$7/8$ cup water
2   tablespoons butter
2   tablespoons sugar
1   teaspoon salt
1   tablespoon poppy seeds
       Finely grated zest of 1 lemon
$1/4$ teaspoon lemon extract
$2^1/4$ cups flour
$1/2$ cup blanched almonds

Spray bread pan lightly with vegetable oil. Add all ingredients in order given. Select Bake Light (or bake white bread) and push start. Allow loaf to cool for 30 minutes or longer before removing from bread pan.

Yields 1 loaf

Bread Machine Chocolate-Mint Bread

1   teaspoon yeast
3/4 cup milk
3   tablespoons butter
1   small egg
1/4 teaspoon mint extract
2 1/4 cups flour
6   tablespoons sugar
3   tablespoons baking cocoa
6   tablespoons chocolate chips
6   tablespoons chopped pecans

Spray bread pan lightly with vegetable oil. Add all ingredients in order given. Select Bake Light (or bake white bread) and push start. Allow loaf to cool for 30 minutes or longer before removing from bread pan.

Yields 1 loaf

Cinnamon Basil Whole Wheat Peach Bread

1   cup all-purpose flour
1   tablespoon baking powder
1/2 teaspoon salt
1/2 teaspoon ground cinnamon
1   cup whole wheat flour
1/3 cup packed brown sugar
1/2 cup chopped pecans
1/2 cup mashed fresh peach
1   cup milk
1/4 cup vegetable oil
1   egg, beaten
1   teaspoon peach extract
2   tablespoons fresh cinnamon basil

Sift all-purpose flour, baking powder, salt and cinnamon in bowl. Add whole wheat flour, brown sugar and pecans; mix well. Make well in center of mixture; set aside. Combine peach, milk, oil, egg and peach extract in bowl; whisk until blended. Add to flour mixture; stir just until moistened. Fold in cinnamon basil. Pour into 3 greased and floured 3x5-inch loaf pans. Bake at 375 degrees for 25 to 30 minutes or until wooden pick inserted in center comes out clean. Cool in pans on rack for 10 minutes. Remove to wire rack to cool completely.

Yields 3 loaves

Sweet Lemon Bouquet Bread

2   cups flour
1¹/₂ teaspoons baking powder
¹/₄ teaspoon salt
1   tablespoon packed lemon thyme
1   tablespoon packed lemon basil
1   cup sugar
6   tablespoons butter, softened
2   eggs
1   tablespoon grated lemon zest
³/₄ cup half-and-half
¹/₂ cup toasted almonds

Sift flour, baking powder and salt together. Mince lemon thyme and lemon basil with sugar in food processor. Cream butter and sugar mixture in mixer bowl until light and fluffy. Beat in eggs 1 at a time. Stir in lemon zest. Add flour mixture and half-and-half alternately to creamed mixture, beating well after each addition. Stir in almonds. Pour into buttered and lightly floured 5x9-inch loaf pan. Bake at 325 degrees for 1 to 1 1/4 hours. Garnish with fresh mint sprigs.

Yields 1 loaf

Petal Cream Spread

This spread is delightful on toast, bagels, or crackers. It also makes a wonderful icing for spice muffins or carrot muffins.

8   ounces cream cheese, softened
¹/₂ cup Fredericksburg
         Edible Flower Preserves

Mix cream cheese with preserves in bowl. Chill thoroughly.

Yields 1 1/4 to 1 1/2 cups

Making Butter Better

Butters are often an overlooked culinary touch; fresh herbs from the garden and butter are unlimited in decadent flavor combinations, and can supply thousands of possible serving ideas! Since fat carries flavor better than any other medium, just a small pat of herb butter goes a long way toward enhancing not only bread, but also meat, fish, poultry, eggs, steamed vegetables, and fresh pasta.

Herb butters can be made with little effort; most herbs are easily creamed into softened butter, while others may require a few minutes in the food processor. They freeze well, too, because the butterfat naturally coats and preserves the ingredients. Tightly covered, they will keep well in the refrigerator for one to two weeks.

Start with unsalted butter to control the amount of salt in the

finished spread and to retain a more delicate flavor. Since unsalted butter is more perishable than salted butter, keep the herb butter frozen if it is not to be used within a week.

As a general rule, use 1/2 cup roughly chopped fresh herbs to 1/2 cup butter. Try a simple butter with 1/2 cup shredded fresh basil combined with 1/2 cup softened unsalted butter. It's excellent with all fresh vegetables and seafood and for sautéing chicken or scrambling eggs.

Herbs to be combined with butter should be freshly cut but without excess moisture (which might cause the spread to mold quickly). After blending, allow flavors to fully develop by refrigerating for at least three hours. As

with any frozen food, the flavor of frozen herb butter is best if it is used within three months.

Experiment with herb blends, combining herbs that you like best and that you think will taste good together. Usually, combinations of two or three herbs provide sufficient balance without the herb flavors clashing.

If you're replacing fresh herbs with dried herbs, use one-third of the amount called for with dried herbs. (The basic rule is one tablespoon fresh herbs for each teaspoon dried herbs.)

Herb butters wrapped in parchment paper and then freshly sliced into rounds for storing in smaller sections are a convenient alternative to packing the butter into plastic molds. To form into a cylinder, place butter in the middle of a sheet of parchment paper; loosely fold the paper in half toward you. Using a baking sheet, push paper so that butter inside rolls back into the fold.

Wrap parchment around butter, tie the ends, and store in the refrigerator or freezer.

To serve at the table, an easy yet attractive idea is to top molded butter with an edible flower. For example, spread a small sheet of plastic wrap over a muffin cup. Place a pansy face down on the plastic, spoon softened butter on top (pressing down gently), lift out the mold using the plastic wrap, turn onto a small plate, and peel off the plastic.

Use herb butter in making pie crusts, too. Try savory herbs for quiches and meat/chicken pies, mild herbs—lemon verbena, rose geranium, cinnamon basil—for fruit pies.

Petal Honey Butter

This butter is great on toast, biscuits, or waffles or used as a base for icing.

1   cup firmly packed rose petals
1/3 cup unsalted butter
1/2 cup honey

Remove white "nail" from rose petals. Combine petals, butter and honey in food processor container. Process until well chopped and mixed. Chill thoroughly.

Yields 1 1/4 to 1 1/2 cups

Chive Butter

A chive butter should not be restricted to potatoes—it is excellent with grilled garden tomatoes, fresh corn, sweet peas, and sum-

mer squash. With the addition of a tablespoon of lemon juice or white wine, it adds a delightful finish to meats and seafood.

1/2 cup snipped chives
1/2 cup unsalted butter, softened

Combine chives and butter in bowl. Chill thoroughly.

Yields 3/4 cup

Cilantro and Pine Nut Butter

1/2 cup unsalted butter, softened
1/2 cup minced fresh cilantro
2   cloves of garlic, minced
1   teaspoon fresh lemon juice
2   tablespoons toasted pine nuts

Combine all ingredients in bowl; mix well. Chill for 3 hours to blend flavors.

Yields 3/4 to 1 cup

The Ichthus Garden

"Honest bread is very well—it's the butter that makes the temptation."
—Douglas Jerrold

Green Herb Butter Blend

A delicate spread for sandwiches, fish, eggs, vegetables, and meats.

1/2 cup salted butter, softened
1 tablespoon chopped fresh chives
1 tablespoon chopped fresh parsley
1 tablespoon chopped fresh tarragon
1 tablespoon chopped fresh chervil

Combine all ingredients in bowl; mix well. Chill for 3 hours to mellow flavors.

Yields 3/4 cup

Sweet Herb Butter

A favorite butter with our bed and breakfast guests—it's wonderful to spread on muffins, pancakes, or pastries.

1/2 cup unsalted butter, softened
2 tablespoons minced fresh lemon balm or lemon verbena
1 tablespoon strawberry jam or marmalade
Grated zest of 1 lemon
1 tablespoon brandy (optional)
2 tablespoons (heaping) toasted almonds or pecans

Combine all ingredients in bowl; mix well. Chill thoroughly.

Yields 3/4 to 1 cup

Sweet Herbal Pepper Butter

A fabulous herb spread.

1/2 cup unsalted butter, softened
1/2 tablespoon Fredericksburg Herbal Pepper Preserves
2 tablespoons minced parsley
1 clove of garlic, minced
2 tablespoons toasted walnuts

Combine all ingredients in bowl; mix well. Chill thoroughly. Serve on crackers, French bread or steamed vegetables.

Yields 1/2 cup

Rosemary Olive Butter

Melt a pat of this butter on grilled meats or fish for last-minute flavor.

1   cup unsalted butter, softened
2   tablespoons coarsely chopped
      fresh rosemary
2   tablespoons Dijon mustard
3   tablespoons oil-cured olives,
      drained, chopped

Combine all ingredients in bowl; mix well. Chill thoroughly.

Yields 1 cup

Lemon Chive Butter

Although this butter is meant to be spread on biscuits, it is also splendid on toast, baked potatoes, roast chicken, and freshly made pasta.

6   tablespoons chopped
      fresh parsley
3   tablespoons snipped fresh chives
2   tablespoons snipped
      fresh tarragon
1   teaspoon grated lemon zest
2   cups unsalted butter, softened
1   tablespoon fresh lemon juice
$^1/_4$ to $^1/_2$ teaspoon salt

Mince herbs with lemon zest in food processor, scraping side of bowl frequently. Add butter, lemon juice and salt; mix well. Turn into crock. Chill, covered tightly, overnight or for up to 3 days. Let stand for 30 minutes before serving.

Yields 2 1/4 cups

Dill and Lemon Butter

1   cup unsalted butter, softened
2   tablespoons coarsely chopped
      fresh dill
3   tablespoons grated lemon zest

Combine all ingredients in bowl; mix well. Chill thoroughly.

Yields 1 cup

In Touch with Massage

From the office to the first date, touch has become taboo. Men are repressed about touching, and women are starved for nonsexual closeness. Add the fear of disease, and it's no wonder many people are, well, hands-offish. What's a body to do? Suggest massage: that smooth ministration of another's fingers. Ahhh—the mind drifts, the body relaxes.

Do you think massage is just a pampering treatment for the rich, or only a prelude to sex? Massage is enjoying newfound attention from all sorts of people. Tired of Westernized medical methodology that treats the symptoms and not the cause of illness, the public's interest in alternatives has done a double-take. As one of the most straightforward and safest forms of alternative therapy,

massage (and its complementary sister, aromatherapy) helps encourage the body to release its own natural healing agents. It's the ancient principle of *vis medicatrix naturae*, "the body heals itself."

Several different styles of hands-on treatment exist, but almost any type of massage systematically manipulates the body's soft tissues, primarily the muscles, to benefit the nervous, muscular, and circulatory systems. Usually this manipulation is performed with the hands, but some forms of massage also use the forearms, elbows, and knees—some even use the feet.

Although scientific documentation is shaky, those "in touch" are adamant: Regular massage can take away muscle tension, cleanse the body of toxins by promoting the flow of lymph (a clear liquid from inflamed body tissue), relieve pain by expanding the blood vessels and increasing circulation, and rid the body of lactic acid buildup (which causes stiffness and cramps in athletes). Psychologically, a rubdown relieves fatigue, reduces tension, calms nerves, and just makes a person feel very, very good.

Isn't a back rub just as effective? No, and yes. Part of the effectiveness of massage stems from the simple act of touching—a back rub can help you relax and may even soothe minor local aches. But the more comprehensive effects of a professional massage are the result of rigorous and systematic routines that will benefit your circulatory, muscular, and nervous systems.

The Indulgence Index

Along with massage's growing popularity comes a new appreciation for its many varieties. No longer is Swedish massage the only treatment requested. Today, dozens of different kinds of massage are available, each with its own technique and philosophy. But the approach hardly need be doctrinaire—many massage therapists create their own hybrids to suit the individual client's body.

~ Swedish massage, invigorating and relaxing, is still the hands-down favorite. The client lies on her back on a padded table, her head supported by a folded towel or a specially designed doughnut-like headrest, her torso covered only by a sheet or a large towel. The massage therapist applies a light oil or lotion to the body, which helps to smooth and soothe the skin. Then the therapist begins with long, gliding strokes, followed by kneading, rolling, and tapping to stimulate circulation and stretch tight, gnarled muscles. The deep rubbing gives the skin a finer texture and increased muscle tone appearance. Say "Jaaah!"

~ Sports massage, a variation on Swedish massage, is indispensable for the serious jock. The focus is on frequently exercised specific muscle groups, including the neck, feet, and upper back. If performed before a workout, such massage can help prevent injury by stretching and loosening muscles, increasing joint flexibility. After activity, it can help relieve soreness.

Quote from The Herb Haus Guest Book

"A little bit of 'Heaven on Earth' is how I feel, with all the wonderful gardens, animals, birds singing, rooster crowing, sleeping in a wonderful twig bed and awakening to all these precious sounds—words cannot describe the feelings of peace I have here. Thank you!"

—Marianne L.

⊰ Medical massage, a close cousin of sports massage, also concentrates on particular body parts. This technique, which should be practiced only by licensed physical therapists, helps treat a wide range of soft-tissue problems: post-fracture and post-surgical swelling, bursitis, and inflamed muscles irritated by sciatica and tendinitis.

⊰ Scalp massage is supposed to release tension, improve circulation, and even promote hair growth. The scalp is vigorously kneaded, without pulling the hair. Honestly, though, who cares about the benefits—wouldn't you like to have someone rubbing their fingers through your hair?

⊰ Rolfing makes use of the deep massage and manipulation "no pain, no gain" principle. It is similar to having a steamroller move methodically over the body.

Rolfers apply sustained hand pressure to their clients in an attempt to stretch, roll, and reposition the connective web-like tissue that sheathes the muscles. Aow! The end result? Better flexibility, increased vitality, and renewed vigor. Some Rolfing recipients even feel they've gotten an inch or two taller!

⊰ Where Rolfing is demanding and aggressive, shiatsu, Japanese "finger pressure," is elegant and nimble. The shiatsu therapist starts by surveying the client's "meridians," the channels of energy that flow through torso and limbs. (Each meridian is said to be connected to particular organs.) By pressing on acupressure points, the shiatsu therapist locates and releases "energy blockages" related to stress and illness. Headaches, tension, constipation, and fatigue are relieved by it. Some say it even preserves beauty and bestows serenity. Since shiatsu involves no oils or rubbing, disrobing isn't necessary. Part of the pleasure derives from the

ritual's softly lit room, soothing music, and comfortable pad on which to recline while the therapist moves from point to point on the body, pressing and stretching.

⊰ Is reflexology a kinky pedicure for deep relaxation and stress relief? But it feels sooo good! Massage is concentrated on the feet and, to a lesser extent, the hands and outer ears. It is based on the ancient idea that the extremities represent a microcosm of the body; particular points on the foot correspond to the liver, another to the knee, and so forth. Science is supportive: One study treating PMS found that after eight weeks of reflexology, women who suffered from premenstrual syndrome experienced a 46 percent drop in their physical and psychological symptoms.

⊰ Laughter, what a great massage for the internal organs!

The positive relationship between good humor and good health is no joke: Muscles are activated, heart rate is increased, and respiration is amplified, with increased oxygen exchange—all similar to the effects of a brisk walk. Muscles in the face, arms, legs, and stomach all get a mini-workout (remember how your stomach ached the last time you laughed really hard?) and so do the diaphragm, the thorax, and the circulatory and endocrine systems. If the average American laughs 15 or more times a day, how was your day? Have you gotten your 15 laughs? One thing which almost all healthy elderly people seem to have in common is a good sense of humor. He who laughs, lasts. So massage yourself! Create healthy ha-ha's! Norman Cousins once said that "Hearty laughter is a good way to jog internally without having to go outdoors."

Quote from The Herb Haus Guest Book

"Overheard in an Orchard:
Said the Robin to the Sparrow,
'I should really like to know,
why these anxious human beings
rush about and worry so,'
Said the Sparrow to the Robin,
'Friend, I think that it must
be, that they have no Heavenly
Father such as cares for
you and me.' You take time to
smell the roses, too!"

—Don and AnnA.

Mother Nature "Nose" Best

There is little doubt that massage's 100-year fight for respectability has paved the way for aromatherapy, a treatment involving essential oils in which massage is integral. If aromatherapy catches on in this country, it could well and truly thrust massage into the mainstream of therapies. The recent avalanche of cosmetic products proclaiming "aroma-therapeutic properties" may lead you to assume that you know exactly what aromatherapy is. Take another whiff! Just because something has a scented oil in it doesn't make it aroma-therapeutic!

Aromatic oils have been used therapeutically since the time of ancient Egypt and Babylon, and later in Greece, but the specialized knowledge of how various essences affect the body and psyche really surfaced in early twentieth century European medical practice. Doctors began rubbing antiseptic and healing oils such as lavender into the skin of World War I burn patients and achieved incredible results. The British turned aromatherapy into a beauty treatment, giving massage therapy and skin treatments.

The basic premise of aromatherapy is that the essential oils are "active" because the "life force" of a plant has been captured by an extremely technical method of distillation. Since the limbic system of the brain (the seat of memory and emotion) is situated directly above the nose, the effects of inhaling the oils can be almost immediate: A chemical reaction in the brain gives rise to a wide range of feelings from tranquility to mild euphoria, depending upon which oils are used.

In aromatherapy massage, where scented botanical oils are mixed in small proportions with the innocuous carrier-massage oil or lotion, not only are the essential oils inhaled but the oils are actually absorbed through the skin into the

In a lifetime, the average American spends 24 years sleeping and has 1,947 nightmares.

blood system during the course of the massage. Their unique aromas fill the air, please the senses, and add a new dimension to the massage experience! Mixes of oil can be prescribed for specific ailments. Juniper, lavender, and lemon all are said to work as cleansing antiseptics. Juniper is also valued as a tonic for the nervous system, while lavender is considered restorative. Eucalyptus soothes, ylang-ylang relaxes, and sandalwood moisturizes and softens the skin.

If the combined powers of smell and touch are to be used to their greatest effect, our noses need to go to new lengths. Fragrance is about more than just smelling good; it can be a healing ritual. In today's automated don't-touch society (where as many as 80 percent of illnesses are thought to be stress-related), aromatic massage is the perfect medium for relaxation.

Pillow Talk

On a good night, sleep tiptoes in, drifting across our consciousness in a gentle wave. At other times, it can be maddeningly elusive, staying just out of reach of a stressed-out mind and overworked body. From our late-night TV talk shows to 24-hour home shopping to the growing number of third shift workers and the need to cram more into each day, sleep is the endangered personal resource of the 90's. No wonder that sleep is the topic of polite chitchat in American offices most mornings. "How much sleep did you get last night?" "If only I could get a few extra hours!" Or the irritating "I need only four hours sleep."

To turn loose of the day's difficulties and tomorrow's worries, just about everyone has a sleeping solution. Ours is to rest your head in Mother Nature's hands. Tuck a little sachet filled with soporific herbs into your pillowcases—every time you stir, you'll take in a relaxing whiff. Sleep pillows aren't just for insomniacs; they're a pleasure for sound sleepers, too. Helpful for waking up on the "right side of the bed," many herbs are believed to promote sweet dreams—and dreaming helps to repair and cleanse a body from fatigue and stress.

Sleep pillows are one of the oldest remedies for encouraging restful sleep. Unlike flower scents, leaf odors are more permanent; they are famous for stuffing, decorating, and strewing. Fresh or dried, herb cuttings have filled cushions, bedding, and little sweet bags to keep things fresh and bug-free. The Romans used rose petals in theirs. King George III (a renowned hypochondriac) and Abraham Lincoln preferred a filling of the papery wild hop blooms, an herb popularized as potent, relaxing, and inducive to sleep. At nap time, Victorian ladies rested on lacy pillows of lavender and rose petals. Christian legend tells us that the baby Jesus lay on a bed of fragrant sleepy-time bracken, a wild herb later called holy cloves (Our Lady's bedstraw, *Gallium verum*). Lady's bedstraw and sweet woodruff (*Gallium odoratum*) were mixed with rushes and straw for filling mattresses— valued for their dried leaf perfume of new-mown hay (coumarin) and for repelling insects. In some parts of the world the filling for a mattress is still composed of dried grasses,

Quote from The Herb Haus Guest Book

hay, or straw which, when newly made, have a sweet meadow scent of their own. It was, and is, a simple step to add to the filling the dried aromatic herbs.

Sleep pillows can be of any size, but traditionally they are small, relatively flat so that they lie smoothly and unobtrusively inside a pillowcase or under a bed pillow. Pillows can be made from fabric remnants with pretty patterns and colors and, if desired, can be trimmed with lace, ruffles, and ribbons. Lacy handkerchiefs are attractive, too. Each pillow is an envelope, designed to hold a separate herb bag (made of muslin, tulle, or another thin fabric), slipped in through the back. The outer pillow should be washable, and the herb bag should be replaced or refreshed when its fragrance fades (every four to six months). Please note that stale herbs may take on unwanted smells that may actually keep you awake

"Four maids reunited here in the fall: A teacher, scientist, a writer, and a Mom (the best title of all!)

They mused on the sweetness and charm of this place

And thought about swiping some basil or mace.

Morning brought fresh bread and sad good-byes

And lots of sappy, sentimental lies.

We hugged each other, and all agreed,

This was the sabbatical we all did need."

—Debra, Dawn, Barbara, and Ann

rather than put you to sleep.

Many herbs have a sedative effect when inhaled, but not all of those are appropriate fillings for sleep pillows—personal perfume preference counts. The flower, leaf, and herb ingredients in the recipe should all be thoroughly dry before using. Be sparing when filling the sachets, so that the finished pillow remains fairly flat; consider the sleeper's comfort. Gently crush the mixture so that no sharp or tough parts remain. Sprinkling the dried herbs with water and a trace of alcohol or glycerin softens them so that they don't rustle and crackle in the pillow when you turn your head.

It's no exaggeration: sleep is one of the pillars of health—when sleep is disturbed, the stability of mind and body is turned upside down. To go to the land of nod, lie down with your hands relaxed at your sides. Close your eyes, begin to breathe easily and naturally, and let your attention follow your breathing. Allow the sleep pillow's aroma to wash over you. You'll begin to notice that just by paying attention to your breathing, your body sinks deeper and deeper into relaxation and your mind becomes quieter, too.

Lemon Pillow

Mix lemon-scented herbs and leaves together in more-or-less equal quantities—include, for example, lemon verbena, lemon balm, lemon thyme, lemon-scented geranium. Use finely chopped lemon peel as a fixative.

An Old-Fashioned Pillow Mix

1   part hop flowers
1   part skullcap leaves
2   parts elderflower
4   parts catmint leaves and flowers

Since hops have an almost acrid odor (like a camp fire of poplar wood), adding to the pillow filling equal amounts of any of the especially fragrant herbs, such as rosemary and lavender (recommended more for headaches) or lemon verbena, saves the night.

Geranium Pillow

4   parts rose-scented or Rober's lemon-rose geranium leaves
1   part lavender, rosemary or hops
1   or 2 drops of rose geranium oil on a small piece of cotton wool for each sachet

The rose and lemon-rose scented geraniums have a reputation for encouraging sleepiness and can be combined with other leaves and spices.

Then God said,
"Behold, I have given you
every herb bearing seed,
which is upon the face
of all the earth, and every tree,
in the which is the fruit
of a tree yielding seed; to you
it shall be for meat.
And to every beast of the
earth, and to every fowl
of the air, and to everything that
creepeth upon the earth,
wherein there is life, I have
given every green herb
for meat: and it was so."

—Genesis 1:29-30

The Cross Garden

In the name of the bee, And of the butterfly, And of the breeze, Amen.
—Envoi, Emily Dickinson (1830–1886)

The Classic Cross Garden

Many ancient gardens took the form of a four-by-four shape, a design that was based on the cosmic cross. Indeed, such a garden was first written of in Genesis:

"A river went out of Eden, to water the garden and from thence it was parted, and became into four heads." In the study of numbers, four is the number of creation, the symbol of nature. There are four winds of heaven, four seasons, and four corners of the earth.

Our walk continues with the Cross Garden chapter, which includes thoughts on fragrances in gardens, some delightful ways to use herbs in spicier foods, and the addictive pleasures of pesto. We also share with you some of our favorite holiday and Christmas delights.

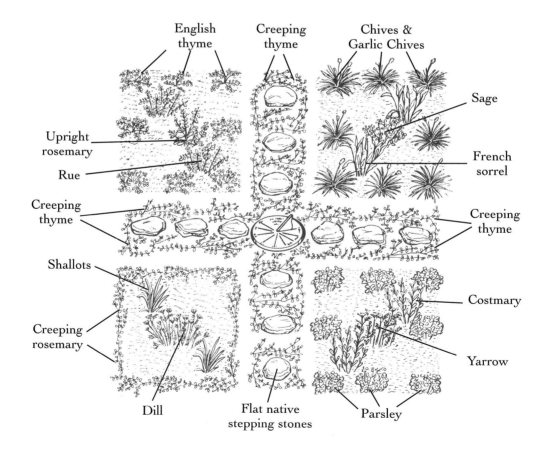

English thyme

Creeping thyme

Chives & Garlic Chives

Sage

Upright rosemary

Rue

French sorrel

Creeping thyme

Creeping thyme

Shallots

Costmary

Creeping rosemary

Yarrow

Dill

Flat native stepping stones

Parsley

A Garden Devoted to Fragrance

By their very nature, herb gardens are rich in fragrances—aromatic, sharp, sweet, often richly pungent. Gerard wrote of mint: ". . . the smell rejoiceth the heart of man. . . ." It's a sensory dessert to walk among herbs on a warm summer's evening, brushing against and pinching leaves, smelling newly opened flowers. Traditionally, the scents of various herbs have their special effects: rosemary and marjoram to cheer and invigorate; mint to refresh the senses; southernwood to increase awareness; hops and lavender to calm the nerves. Gardens rich in scent captivate the mind and are the most memorable.

The warm stillness of a south-facing or west-facing slope provides shelter from wind that would drive the scent away and creates the higher temperatures necessary for many plants to release their aromatic bouquets. A screen of climbing honeysuckle, jasmine, or hops, and/or a scented hedge such as sweetbrier, old roses, lavender, rosemary, or santolina will help to create a paradise-scented stillness.

Paths are frequently considered solely as a way of getting from one part of the yard to another and thus are often neglected. They can become ribbons of perfume—packed plants that create scent and color both at ground level and around one's head.

A garden of herbs grown particularly for their scent should also have small or narrow beds, for easy touching—nibbling for the adventurous—and a destination seat, if possible, with some nearby raised beds or pots for low-growing or delicate plants.

While rather ordered rows may suit culinary or medicinal herbs—herbs with a working purpose—sweet-scented herbs could be grown in a more informal garden style, in pleasing disorder. For those gardeners desiring a traditional landscape, plant small beds divided by paths or low box hedges. Or form a garden shape—such as a large wheel, a divided square, or a ladder. If a large herb garden packed with many aromatic plants is an impossibility, arrange a cluster of pots on a patio or balcony. Fortunately, many herbs are quite content in small containers, and pots with planting holes in the side can be used to accommodate several different types at the same time.

Plant Perfumes

Plant	Scent	Site
Basils — *Ocimum basilicum*	Strongly clove-like	In garden or large pot
Bergamot — *Monarda didyma*	Sweet flowery aroma	In a perennial border
Chamomile — *Chamaemelum nobile*	Sweet mix of bananas and apples	As a fragrant lawn, and at the sides of paths
Clove carnation — *Dianthus caryophyllus*	Clove-like and sweet	Along path edges and perennial borders
Geraniums —		
Almond — *P. quericifolium*	Almond-scented leaves	On a kitchen window or in a cool room
Lemon — *P. crispum*	Lemon and balm-like leaves	On a kitchen window or in a cool room
Nutmeg — *P. x fragrans*	Nutmeg and pine-scented leaves	On a kitchen window or in a cool room
Peppermint — *P. tomentosum*	Strongly peppermint leaves	On a kitchen window or in a cool room
Rose — *P. graveolens*	Rose-scented leaves	On a kitchen window or in a cool room
Honeysuckle — *Lonicera japonica*	Sweet	Over rustic poles and fences
L. periclymenum	Sweet	Over rustic poles and fences
L. sempervirens	Sweet	Over rustic poles and fences
Hyssop — *Hyssopus officinalis*	Bitter and mint-like	In an herb garden or in pots
Jasmine — *Jasminum polyanthum*	Sweet	Over a frame in a porch (suitable in mild areas)
Jasminum humile	Sweet	Up a warm facing wall
Jasminum x stephanese	Sweet	Trailing over archways
Lavender — *Lavandula officinalis*	Air-drenching aroma	Adaptable plant ideal between roses/as a hedge
Lavandula stoechas	Intense fragrance	Edging for border/against brick wall
Lemon balm — *Melissa officinalis*	Fresh lemon scent	In an herb garden or perennial border

Plant Perfumes

Plant	Scent	Site
Lemon verbena—*Aloysia triphylla*	Strong lemon scent, especially bruised	Suitable outside only in warm areas
Marjoram/Oregano—*Origanum vulgare*	Sweet, balsam-like leaves, warm, bitter	In an herb garden or pot
Mints—Corsican—*Mentha requienii*	Peppermint-scented leaves	In herb garden/pots
French—*Mentha x villosa*	Fruity, strongly mint-scented	In herb garden/bucket to restrict roots
Peppermint—*Mentha x poperita*	Strongly peppermint-scented leaves	In herb garden/bucket
Spearmint—*Mentha spicata*	Strongly mint-scented	In herb garden/bucket
Mock Orange—*Ph. microphyllus*	Sweet and orangey	Plant in a shrub border
Philadelphus microphyllus	Richly sweet orange	Ideal for small garden, alongside a path
Orange Blossom— *Avalanche Philadephus*	Orange blossom-like and richly sweet	Ideal in a mixed or shrub border
Rose—*Cecile Brunner*	Light fragrant flowers	Compact bush form
Marquise Boccella	Light sweet scent	Neat erect plant
Penelope	Intense musk-rose perfume	Superb for hedging
Sombreuil	Delicious tea rose fragrance	Ideal as pillar rose/train on fence/trellis
Souvenir de la Malmaison	Known as the "Queen of Beauty and Fragrance"	Bush grows up to 3 ft.; nice fit for any garden
Rosemary—*Rosmarinus officinalis*	Peppery, seacoast-scent of pine	Large tub on patio/plant as a border
Sweet woodruff—*Galium odoratum*	Sweet hay scent increases as herb dries	At edges of paths
Thyme—*Thymus serpyllum*	Sweet pungent-plummy earth scent	Alongside paths and for aromatic lawn
T. x citriodorus	Pungent and lemony	Along path edges
T. herba-barona	Pungent sweet caraway	Path edges/ground cover
Violet—*Viola odorata*	Very sweet perfume	Paths/rock gardens/pots

The rose looks fair,
but fairer we it deem
for that sweet odour
which doth in it live.
—Shakespeare, Sonnets

All Fired Up: Herbs for Salsa

If you've thought of salsas as just chopped up tomatoes and peppers (with a little cilantro thrown in sometimes), think again. Not exactly condiments, yet not quite side dishes, salsas are a combination of fresh vegetables and/or fruits, herbs, chiles, and spices. Although salsas can vary widely in ingredients, taste, color, and texture, they are similar in that their flavors are meant to be intense—sometimes sweet, sour, hot, or earthy. Yes, salsas do add flavor—lighting up every taste bud in your mouth—but without harming our health, as they contain little fat or cholesterol. Also, since most of them use raw ingredients (such as chile peppers, vinegar, herbs, and spices), their recipes call for no more culinary equipment or skill than a sharp knife and the ability to chop and stir! For the herb gardener and cook, preparing salsa gives us a good excuse to add an herb we've been wanting to taste. When temperatures begin to climb, it makes "scents" to cool off with the tasty addition of salsa to steaks, pork, or chicken; to vegetables such as green beans, zucchini, and summer squash; to scrambled eggs; and to chips as an appetizer.

Rosemary-Thyme Salsa

1	tomato, chopped
1/4	cup chopped red onion
2	tablespoons minced chives
2	small jalapeño peppers, seeded, chopped
1	tablespoon fresh thyme leaves
1	tablespoon minced fresh rosemary
1/8	teaspoon salt
1 1/2	tablespoons white wine
1 1/2	tablespoons red wine vinegar
1 1/2	tablespoons olive oil
1	teaspoon Tabasco sauce

Combine tomato, onion, chives, jalapeño peppers, thyme, rosemary, salt, wine, vinegar, olive oil and Tabasco sauce in skillet. Simmer over medium heat for 15 minutes, stirring occasionally. Serve warm or at room temperature. May substitute basil and tarragon or dill and savory for thyme and rosemary.

Yields 8 (2-ounce) servings

Avocado and Corn Salsa with Oregano

3   ears corn, husked
2   avocados, peeled and chopped
1   red onion, finely chopped
1   red bell pepper, finely chopped
2   tablespoons olive oil
1/3 cup red wine vinegar
1   tablespoon finely minced garlic
1   tablespoon ground cumin
1   teaspoon red pepper flakes
1/4 cup chopped fresh oregano
1/4 cup fresh lime juice
    Salt and coarsely ground black
       pepper to taste

Blanch corn in boiling water in saucepan for 3 minutes. Drain and cool under cold water. Cut kernels from cobs into medium bowl. Add avocados, onion, bell pepper, olive oil, vinegar, garlic, cumin, red pepper flakes, oregano, lime juice, salt and black pepper. Mix well. Chill overnight for best flavor. May substitute fresh marjoram, savory or thyme for oregano.

Yields 17 (2-ounce) servings

Avocado Appetizer

1   large avocado, chopped
3/4 cup prepared Fredericksburg
       Herbal Salsa

Combine avocado and Herbal Salsa in small bowl; mix well. Spoon 1 rounded teaspoonful of mixture onto whole wheat crackers. Garnish with bacon bits.

Yields 10 (1-ounce) servings

Cheesy Herb Crunch

5   tablespoons margarine
1/2 teaspoon salt
6   cups Chex cereal
1   packet Fredericksburg Herb 'N
       Cheddar Popcorn Seasoning

Melt margarine in large skillet over low heat. Sprinkle with salt. Add cereal, stirring until coated. Cook until cereal is lightly toasted, stirring frequently. Sprinkle with Popcorn Seasoning, stirring to coat. Serve in basket lined with absorbent paper.

Yields 6 (1-cup) servings

Cheesy Herbed French Bread

1   loaf French bread
1/2   cup butter, softened
3   tablespoons Fredericksburg
       Herb 'N Cheddar
       Popcorn Seasoning
1   clove of garlic, crushed
1/4   teaspoon Fredericksburg
       Lemon Pepper
1/8   teaspoon cayenne

Slice bread diagonally, but do
not cut through bottom of crust.
Combine butter, Popcorn
Seasoning, garlic, Lemon Pepper
and cayenne in small bowl; mix
well. Spread mixture on bread
slices. Place on baking sheet.
Sprinkle bread with a few drops of
water. Bake at 350 degrees for 10
minutes. Serve immediately.

Yields 16 slices

Herb Toasts

Accompanied by a salad, these
bread rounds make a delicious
lunch or appetizer.

1/2   cup sour cream
8   ounces cream cheese, softened
1   large green onion, minced
2   tablespoons (heaping)
       Fredericksburg
       Herbs de Provence
2   large cloves of garlic, minced
2/3   cup chopped pecans
1   loaf French bread, thinly sliced
1/4   cup extra-virgin olive oil

Beat sour cream, cream cheese,
green onion, Herbs de Provence,
garlic and pecans in small bowl
until light and fluffy; set aside.
Place bread slices on baking
sheet. Brush with olive oil. Toast in
oven on both sides; cool. Spread
generously with cheese mixture.
Broil until cheese and bread are
heated through. Garnish with
parsley. Arrange on large platter
with centerpiece of red and green
grapes to serve.

Yields 24 servings

Syl's Dilly Dip Canapes

1   loaf white bread, crusts trimmed
1   cup Syl's Dilly Dip
3   ounces freshly grated
       Parmesan cheese

Cut bread into decorative shapes
with cookie cutter. Place on
baking sheet. Toast on one side.
Prepare Dilly Dip using package
directions. Spread on untoasted
side of bread; sprinkle with
cheese. Chill, covered, until serving
time. Broil in oven until lightly
browned. May substitute any
other cheese for Parmesan cheese
and sprinkle tops with dried
rosemary or basil before broiling.

Yields 24 servings

Creamy Vegetable Dip

1/4   cup chopped parsley
2   tablespoons chopped chives
1   egg
1   clove of garlic, minced
1   teaspoon lemon juice
1/2   teaspoon Fredericksburg Vinegar
1/2   teaspoon mustard
1/4   teaspoon salt
1/2   teaspoon Fredericksburg
        Herb and Pepper Seasoning
1/8   teaspoon Tabasco sauce
        or to taste
1/4   teaspoon lemon pepper
3/4   cup Fredericksburg Olive Oil

Combine parsley, chives, egg, garlic,
lemon juice, Vinegar, mustard,
salt, Herb and Pepper Seasoning,
Tabasco sauce and lemon pepper
in blender container. Process until
well mixed. Add Olive Oil slowly
while blender is running, allowing
sauce to thicken as oil is added.

Yields 8 (1-ounce) servings

Pizza Garden

Create your own pizza
garden by planting the herbs
you use to make
pizza in a twelve-inch pot.

This might include basil,
thyme, marjoram, parsley, and
oregano. Snip as needed.

Nacho Supreme

1   large tortilla chip
1   slice Cheddar cheese
1/2   teaspoon prepared
        Fredericksburg Herbal Salsa
1/2   teaspoon sour cream
1   teaspoon chopped scallions
1   teaspoon chopped black olives

Layer tortilla chip with cheese,
Herbal Salsa, sour cream,
scallions and olives. Garnish
with slice of jalapeño pepper.
Place on microwave-safe plate.
Microwave on High for 20 to
30 seconds, or broil on rack of
broiler pan until bubbly.

Yields 1 serving

Basil-Tomato Pizza

2   tablespoons olive oil
1   large onion, chopped
1   large tomato, chopped
3   large cloves of garlic, minced
1/4 cup chopped fresh basil
     Salt and pepper to taste
1   recipe pizza dough
1 3/4 cups shredded Provolone cheese
3/4 cup grated Parmesan cheese
1/4 cup chopped fresh basil

Heat oil in small skillet. Sauté onion until tender but not browned. Add tomato and garlic. Cook for 10 minutes or until liquid evaporates, stirring occasionally. Mix in 1/4 cup basil, salt and pepper. Line pizza pan with pizza dough. Spread tomato mixture evenly over pastry to within 1/2 inch of edge. Top with cheeses. Bake at 425 degrees for 20 minutes or until crust is golden. Sprinkle with basil before serving.

Yields 6 servings

Entertaining— a Piece of Pizza

Some ninety acres of pizza are consumed every day in the U.S., and it need not be off limits to those sticking to a New Year's resolution to watch their waistlines.

Serving pizza to your weight-conscious friends is an easy form of entertaining, too.

Let your guests make their own pizzas—set up a table loaded with sauces, toppings, and herb and flower garnishes.

Make your crusts small so that each guest has a chance to sample a variety of robust and mild flavors.

Three-Pepper Oregano Pizza

2   tablespoons olive oil
1   large red bell pepper,
       cut into 1/2-inch slices
1   large green bell pepper,
       cut into 1/2-inch slices
1   large yellow bell pepper,
       cut into 1/2-inch slices
2   tablespoons chopped
       fresh oregano
1/2 teaspoon salt
1   recipe pizza dough
1   cup shredded mozzarella cheese

Heat oil in medium skillet. Sauté bell peppers until tender-crisp. Season with oregano and salt. Line pizza pan with pizza dough; sprinkle with half the cheese. Spoon pepper mixture evenly over cheese. Top with remaining cheese. Bake at 425 degrees for 20 minutes or until crust is golden brown.

Yields 6 servings

Pesto Perfect

Once experienced, pesto must be one of the world's most addictive culinary pleasures. Pesto is usually a combination of fresh herbs, olive oil, a sharp hard cheese, garlic cloves, and pine nuts blended into a thick paste. However, other ingredients, such as unsalted butter, orange or lemon peel, sugar, and other fresh herbs, should also be considered by the adventurous cook for blending sweet pestos.

The name "pesto" derives from the word "pestle," the implement used to grind herbs and other ingredients into a paste. Today, convenient food processors and blenders usually replace the more time-consuming mortar and pestle in making this uncooked seasoning, with virtually no loss of the fresh herb's flavor.

Why bother making this unusual seasoning? Pesto is a

perfectly delicious and foolproof way of concentrating an herb's intense flavor in a form which can, with proper storage, be enjoyed year round. Moreover, with so many plentiful herbs, especially basil, summer is an ideal time to make up several large batches to keep in the freezer for later use or for unusual gifts.

A whole range of herb pastes from spicy to sweet can be made by combining a variety of herbs, fresh greens, oils, and nuts. Even in preparing a classic basil pesto, there are no set rules. Some versions include cream, others butter; some use cheese from sheep's milk, others a combination of Romano and Parmesan cheeses, or Parmesan alone.

You should always start with fine, fresh ingredients, as the seasoning will only be as good as the ingredients going into it. Harvesting your herbs in the morning before the sun heats up and dissipates the herbs' natural oils is best.

If you are using herbs that don't provide a lot of green bulk, as with thyme, or if you are substituting dried for fresh herbs in a recipe, add a "green extender" for flavor, color, and texture. Italian flat parsley, spinach, kale, watercress, or sorrel works well. These greens dilute the flavor and intensity of the herb, and in the case of robust ones such as rosemary and thyme, this is desirable. Cheese purchased in bulk and freshly grated will give the pesto its fullest flavor.

Choosing an oil is also important. A virgin olive oil should be adequate. The extra-virgin olive oil will make a quality pesto, although a pesto made with strong-scented herbs may overpower the benefits of this oil's fruity flavor. Pure olive oil is not recommended, as its aftertaste tends to be too strong. Pine nuts are a classic addition to a pesto, and toasting them will give a stronger, nuttier flavor. Be adventurous and try other nuts—macadamia nuts, pistachios, walnuts, pecans, or even sunflower seeds. However, delicate pestos, using a mild herb such as tarragon, really need a blander, unsalted nut.

Pestos will keep well in the refrigerator for three to four weeks. Pack the seasoning in small containers; cover with a thin layer of olive oil or unsalted butter and cap tightly. Remove as much air as possible to prevent loss of the pesto's color and flavor. Some discoloration on the surface will not affect the flavor; simply stir this part into the green below and add

another layer of oil. When freezing in quantities, it is not necessary to cover the pesto with oil. Pesto will keep for six to eight months in the freezer.

Using pestos is easy and rewarding. Pesto and pasta are a classic duo. Add a few tablespoons of the water used to cook the pasta to thin the pesto, and then toss with hot pasta. Allow about 1 cup pesto for each pound of pasta. Alternatively, add a tablespoon or two of pesto to a soup, sauce, or sautéed vegetable, or combine with the juices of meat, chicken, or fish for an elegant basting sauce. Adding milk or cream creates a superb sauce for any main dish. For a quick snack, lightly spread pesto on soda crackers, top with freshly grated Parmesan cheese and chopped tomatoes, and heat if desired. And don't forget what a lovely addition sweet pestos are for filling cakes and cookies, or for combining with crumb toppings and frostings.

Basic Pesto

Menu pictured on page 42.

3 cups fresh basil
4 to 6 cloves of garlic
1/2 to 3/4 cup freshly grated Parmesan cheese
2 to 3 tablespoons freshly grated Romano cheese
1/2 cup pine nuts, walnuts or pecans
2/3 cup olive oil
Salt and pepper to taste

Chop basil and garlic in food processor. Add cheeses and pine nuts. Process, adding olive oil slowly, until thoroughly mixed. Season with salt and pepper. Spoon into small jars and seal with thin layer of olive oil or melted butter. Store in refrigerator or freezer. For a nuttier flavor, lightly toast pine nuts before adding to mixture.

Yields 5 to 6 cups

Sweet Pepper Pesto Corn Bread

This recipe was contributed by Dee Lakari.

1 teaspoon cayenne
$^1/_4$ teaspoon crushed red pepper
$^1/_2$ teaspoon crushed garlic
$^1/_4$ teaspoon cumin
$^1/_2$ tablespoon minced onion
Salt to taste
3 sprigs of Mexican oregano
1 tablespoon chopped purple opal basil
2 tablespoons chopped sweet basil
2 to 3 tablespoons vegetable oil
$2^1/_2$ cups flour
$1^1/_2$ cups cornmeal
$^1/_4$ cup sugar
4 teaspoons baking powder
$^1/_2$ cup vegetable oil
3 eggs, beaten
$^1/_2$ teaspoon baking soda
2 cups sour cream

Purée cayenne, red pepper, garlic, cumin, onion, salt, oregano, basils, and 2 to 3 tablespoons oil in food processor; set aside. Combine flour, cornmeal, sugar and baking powder in large bowl. Make well in center. Stir in 1/2 cup oil and eggs. Mix baking soda with sour cream in small bowl. Add to batter, stirring well. Mix 1 cup batter with pesto mixture; set aside. Pour remaining batter into greased 9x13-inch glass baking dish. Swirl in pesto batter. Bake at 350 degrees for 20 to 25 minutes or until golden brown.

Yields 12 servings

Pesto Spread or Dip

4 medium cloves of garlic
1 (10-ounce) package frozen spinach, thawed and drained
1 cup chopped fresh parsley
$^3/_4$ cup pine nuts or pecans
1 cup freshly grated Parmesan cheese
$^1/_4$ cup chopped green onions
1 teaspoon salt
$^1/_4$ cup Fredericksburg Pesto Seasoning
$1^1/_4$ cups (approximately) olive oil

Mince garlic finely in food processor. Add spinach, parsley, pine nuts, cheese, green onions, salt and Pesto Seasoning. Process until well mixed. Add olive oil gradually while processor is running to obtain desired consistency. Store, covered, in refrigerator for up to 1 week or freeze for up to 3 months. Bring to room temperature to serve, stirring well. Spread on crackers or toasted bread and garnish with chopped tomatoes or freshly grated Parmesan cheese.

Yields 6 cups

Pesto Baklava

2   cups packed fresh basil leaves
4   large cloves of garlic
1   cup freshly grated
     Parmesan cheese
1/4 cup freshly grated
     Romano cheese
1   cup chopped pecans
1/2 teaspoon salt
1/4 teaspoon pepper
1/2 cup olive oil
1   (16-ounce) package
     phyllo pastry
2   cups melted butter

Combine basil, garlic, cheeses, pecans, salt and pepper in food processor container. Process until thoroughly mixed. Add olive oil gradually while processor is running until mixture is of desired consistency; set aside. Cut phyllo leaves into halves to fit a 9x13-inch glass dish. Keep phyllo leaves covered with plastic or dampened towel to keep moist. Place one sheet of phyllo in buttered baking dish; brush with butter. Repeat until 14 sheets of pastry have been used, buttering each sheet. Spread 1 cup pesto filling over pastry layers. Repeat layering and buttering of 14 sheets of pastry topped with pesto until all ingredients have been used. Cut into serving pieces. Bake at 325 degrees for 1 hour and 20 minutes or until golden brown. Let stand for 20 minutes before removing from pan.

Yields 32 servings

Green Pesto

Menu pictured on page 42.

4   cloves of garlic
1   (10-ounce) package frozen
     spinach, thawed and drained
1   cup fresh parsley leaves
1/2 cup pine nuts
3/4 cup freshly grated
     Parmesan cheese
1/4 cup chopped fresh chives
1   teaspoon salt
1   cup olive oil

Mince garlic in food processor. Add spinach, parsley, pine nuts, cheese, chives and salt. Process until thoroughly mixed. Add olive oil gradually while processor is running until desired consistency is obtained. Store, covered, in refrigerator for up to 1 week or freeze for up to 3 months. Bring to room temperature before serving.

Yields 5 cups

Chicken Spinach Salad with Green Pesto Dressing

1/4 cup chopped pecans
1 clove of garlic, minced
1/4 teaspoon salt
1 tablespoon olive oil
1 cup light mayonnaise
1 tablespoon (heaping)
    Green Pesto
2 cups chopped cooked chicken
1 cup fresh spinach, torn
2 tablespoons chopped black olives

Sauté pecans and garlic with salt in hot oil in skillet until golden; cool. Mix mayonnaise and Green Pesto (page 58) in large bowl. Stir in chicken, spinach, olives and pecan mixture. Serve at room temperature. Garnish with additional Green Pesto.

Yields 4 servings

Vegetable Pesto Bread

Enlivened with savory herbs and vegetable juice, this unusual bread is quite good spread with cream cheese, or for interesting sandwiches. Its distinctive tawny gold color makes a handsome addition to any table.

3 1/2 to 4 cups all-purpose unbleached
    flour
1 envelope fast-rising dry yeast
1 tablespoon sugar
3 tablespoons chopped fresh
    parsley leaves
2 teaspoons dried basil leaves
1/2 teaspoon salt
1/4 teaspoon celery salt
1/8 teaspoon red pepper flakes
1/8 teaspoon garlic powder
1 cup vegetable juice cocktail
2 tablespoons vegetable oil
1 egg white
1 tablespoon water
1 tablespoon grated
    Parmesan cheese

Combine 1 cup flour, yeast, sugar, parsley, basil, salt, celery salt, red pepper flakes and garlic powder in food processor container fitted with steel blade. Process for 5 seconds to mix. Heat vegetable juice and oil to 125 to 130 degrees in small saucepan. Start food processor and add juice mixture quickly, processing for 10 seconds. Add 2 1/4 cups flour. Process for 7 to 8 seconds or until dough forms a ball. Turn out onto floured surface. Knead in enough remaining flour until dough becomes smooth and elastic. Place in greased bowl, turning to grease surface. Let rise, covered, in warm place for 20 minutes. Punch down and knead for 5 minutes. Shape into round loaf. Place on greased round baking pan. Let rise, covered, for 20 minutes longer. Brush with mixture of egg white and water; sprinkle with Parmesan cheese. Cut a 1/2-inch deep and 4-inch long cross in top of loaf with sharp knife. Bake at 375 degrees for 30 to 35 minutes or until browned and loaf tests done. Cool on wire rack.

Yields 1 loaf

Wrapping Up Gifts

To make the prettiest
and most personal gift wraps,
tie your presents with
ribbon or green floral string
and sprigs of fresh herbs.

Write the meaning of
the herbs on a card glued to
the back of the gift:
Rosemary—remembrance
or your presence revives me;
myrtle—love;
ivy—constancy and friendship;
rose geranium—preference;
marjoram—blushes and happiness;
sage—domestic virtue
and immortality;
rose buds—young love;
statice—everlasting.

Bread Wreaths—the Ultimate Comfort Food

Round, full, complete, an anticipation of celebration: A bread wreath gives us a perfect simple feast, especially when it's freshly baked, buttered, and accompanied by a cup of tea. An herb wreath brings to man, woman, and child a physical sense of continuity and God's presence. And beyond this fulfillment, a baked bread's sweet-grain aroma evokes something during the struggle against seasonal elements that nothing else does—perhaps a tummy-warm reassurance of change. A braided golden herb bread wreath looks—and tastes— like comfort food should. Too pretty to eat? Let it dry, lacquer it, and use it as the breakfast table centerpiece for the duration of the damp, chill, and bluster. But please do bake another to feast upon!

Holiday Bread Wreath

When making wreaths of bread, count on each one having its own unique shape. Like family and friends, no two will be alike—one may be fat, one thin, one lopsided— but delightful just the same.

1/3 cup unsalted butter
1/4 cup minced fresh parsley
1   tablespoon fresh thyme leaves
1   teaspoon minced fresh sage
1/4 teaspoon minced fresh rosemary
1   tablespoon freshly grated onion
1/4 teaspoon ground white pepper
2   cups whole wheat flour
1 1/2 cups bread flour
1   teaspoon salt
2   tablespoons sugar
2   tablespoons nonfat dry milk powder
*2 1/2 teaspoons 50% faster active
        dry yeast*
1 1/4 cups hot water
1/2 cup minced fresh parsley
*2   tablespoons melted
        unsalted butter*
1/4 cup walnut pieces

Combine 1/3 cup butter, 1/4 cup parsley, thyme, sage, rosemary, onion and pepper in saucepan. Cook over medium heat for 1 minute, stirring frequently. Remove from heat and set aside. Combine wheat flour, bread flour, salt, sugar, milk powder and yeast in food processor container. Process for 1 to 2 minutes or until well mixed. Add herb-infused butter and hot water while processor is running. Process until dough forms a ball. Remove to floured surface and knead for several minutes to remove air bubbles. Shape dough into a ball and place in lightly greased bowl, turning to grease surface. Cover with damp towel. Let rise in warm place for 45 minutes or until doubled in bulk. Remove to lightly floured surface; knead in remaining 1/2 cup parsley. Divide dough into 3 equal portions. Shape each portion into a 12-inch long rope. Place ropes parallel on greased and floured baking sheet. Braid together, pinching ends to seal; shape into desired wreath form. Brush with melted butter; sprinkle with walnuts. Let rise, covered, in warm place for 35 minutes or until doubled in bulk. Bake at 350 degrees for 35 to 45 minutes or until bread is golden brown and sounds hollow when tapped. Cool on wire rack. Wrap in plastic wrap to store.

Yields 12 servings

A Christmas Eve Menu

For us, one of the most memorable parts of the Christmas season is our Christmas Eve meal. It's a time of high anticipation for the following day's fellowship, as well as a time of hectic, last-minute gift wrapping. Out of necessity, the meal must be fast and easy, yet festive enough to contribute to the spirited occasion. Most of the following menu can be made a few days early and chilled, and it may even taste better after a second warming.

Festive herb punch

Tossed green salad with mustard vinaigrette

Herbed lamb pie

Green peas with minted garlic butter

Rosemary-spiced cranberries

Ginger lemon bars

Festive Herb Punch

2	large bunches lemon balm
2	large bunches mint
1	(46-ounce) can unsweetened fruit juice
	Juice of 2 lemons
1	lemon, thinly sliced
1	quart sparkling water

Place lemon balm and mint bunches in large glass pitcher. Pour in fruit juice, lemon juice and lemon slices. Chill overnight, stirring occasionally and pressing down herbs with wooden spoon. Pour into chilled glasses with a splash of sparkling water. Garnish with sprigs of fresh lemon balm and/or mint.

Yields 8 servings

Tossed Green Salad with Mustard Vinaigrette

1/4	cup Dijon mustard
1	tablespoon lemon juice
2/3	cup whipping cream
2	tablespoons minced fresh parsley
2	teaspoons minced shallot
1	head romaine or other lettuce, torn

Whisk mustard and lemon juice in small bowl. Add cream gradually, whisking constantly until thickened. Stir in parsley and shallot. Drizzle over lettuce in salad bowl, tossing to coat.

Yields 6 servings

Herbed Lamb Pie

2 cups chopped onion
3 cloves of garlic, minced
2 tablespoons butter
1 pound ground lamb
1/2 cup boiling water
1/2 teaspoon ground allspice
1/2 teaspoon salt
   Freshly ground
      black pepper to taste
1 tablespoon minced
      fresh rosemary
1/4 cup chopped fresh parsley
1 recipe (2-crust) pie pastry
1 egg
2 tablespoons milk

Sauté onion and garlic in butter in large skillet for 5 minutes, stirring frequently. Add lamb. Cook over low heat, stirring until browned and crumbly. Add water, allspice, salt, pepper and rosemary. Simmer, partially covered, for 40 minutes. Stir in parsley; remove from heat. Line 9-inch pie plate with half the pie pastry. Spoon in lamb mixture evenly. Cover with remaining pastry, sealing edge and perforating with fork. Brush with mixture of egg and milk. Bake at 450 degrees for 10 minutes; reduce oven temperature to 350 degrees. Bake for 40 minutes longer.

Yields 6 servings

Green Peas with Minted Garlic Butter

3 cloves of garlic
1/2 cup butter, softened
2 tablespoons minced fresh parsley
1 tablespoon minced fresh mint
16 ounces fresh or frozen green peas

Boil garlic in water to cover in saucepan for 4 to 5 minutes. Drain well and dry; crush in small bowl. Cream butter in mixer bowl until light and fluffy. Add garlic, parsley and mint, beating well. Chill, covered, for several hours before using. Cook peas until tender; drain. Place in serving dish; dot with herb butter.

Yields 6 servings

Rosemary-Spiced Cranberries

2 cups sugar
3/4 cup water
4 cups cranberries
1 teaspoon freshly grated nutmeg
1/2 teaspoon crushed cardamom pods
1/2 teaspoon ground allspice
2 teaspoons minced fresh rosemary

Cook sugar and water in heavy saucepan over medium heat until sugar dissolves, stirring constantly. Bring to a boil. Add cranberries, nutmeg, cardamom, allspice and rosemary. Cook for 10 minutes or until cranberries pop. Remove from heat to cool. Refrigerate, covered, until serving time. Serve warm or at room temperature. Garnish with fresh rosemary sprigs.

Yields 8 servings

Ginger Lemon Bars

3/4 cup unsalted butter, softened
1/3 cup confectioners' sugar
1 teaspoon lemon balm
1/3 cup minced crystallized ginger
3/4 teaspoon ground ginger
1 1/2 cups flour
3 eggs
1 1/3 cups sugar
1 teaspoon lemon balm
6 tablespoons lemon juice
3 tablespoons flour
1/2 teaspoon baking powder
1/4 teaspoon salt
3 tablespoons confectioners' sugar

Cream butter and 1/3 cup confectioners' sugar in mixer bowl until light and fluffy. Add 1 teaspoon lemon balm, crystallized ginger and ground ginger; mix thoroughly. Add 1 1/2 cups flour gradually, beating well after each addition. Spread mixture in 9x13-inch baking pan. Bake at 350 degrees for 12 to 15 minutes or until golden brown. Whisk eggs, sugar, 1 teaspoon lemon balm, lemon juice, 3 tablespoons flour, baking powder and salt in bowl. Pour over prepared crust. Bake for 15 to 20 minutes or until firm. Sift 3 tablespoons confectioners' sugar over top; cool. Cut into bars to serve.

Yields 24 bars

As aromatic plants bestow, No spicy fragrance while they grow;
But crush'd or trodden to the ground, Diffuse their balmy sweets around.
—Oliver Goldsmith

Holiday Herbal Desserts

Desserts prepared with herbs are tempting all year long, but they are somehow most evocative of Christmastime, when the richer, the more sumptuous and extravagant the approach, the better. Classic ingredient favorites—nuts and dried fruits, cranberries, custards, apples, chocolate, and eggnog—for holiday indulgences are made even more special by the unmistakable assertive sensation of an herb at its freshest. Herbs definitely have a festive quality. Their varied green hues and textures, fragrances, and flavors, as well as legends associated with the story of Christmas, inspire me in recipes. Simple custards, cookies and tarts, baked fruits, and puddings all take on a subtle sophistication thanks to the small addition of some common herbs available in your winter garden or indoor hanging baskets.

It took me a bit of trial-and-error time to gain confidence in cooking with herbs, though, because they can be a temperamental ingredient. First, I had to learn something that may seem obvious: always use an herb that is fit to eat! Taste (nibble) the herb (fresh or dried) before using it. This is particularly critical when the herb will not be cooked into a dessert; for example, if it is only sprinkled on top. But it's also important when the herb is cooked into a dish. Herbs leave a definite flavor behind, and you'll want that taste to be top quality. In general, when adding herbs to a favorite dessert of your own, I suggest starting with one teaspoon minced fresh leaves per four-serving recipe. Add more according to your taste.

Second, for some sweets it is best to use an herb that adds complementary notes to the dish, rather than similar flavors. Date Nut Pudding scented with the peppery-pine fragrance of rosemary provides a delightful counterpoint to the orange Grand Marnier sauce. The lemon peel-camphor notes of culinary sage enliven a mixture of poached prunes and apple, and the cinnamon dumplings served with it round out the soft muskiness of the herb. I've always liked cookies and custards, so I'm partial to the crisp and elegant lemon balm cornucopias which spill over with tangy herb fresh custard and marinated minted berries.

When I want to let other flavors prevail, I'll sprinkle a minced herb as a garnish to add character to the dessert's appearance rather than to its flavor. The festive Cranberry Cream Cheese Tart with Orange Crust doesn't need another layer of flavor, so a mild herb like mint fills the bill for accessorizing the red and white tart with green.

Of course, an herb-scented beverage can also be a dessert in itself, especially if it adds fragrance to a full-bodied ginger-geranium eggnog (steep one

bruised leaf per cup of eggnog a day in advance in the refrigerator) or a rich peppermint cocoa (swirl one three-inch mint sprig in each cup of cocoa). To some tastes, a warm brew of mulled wine is a complete finish, but I like to offer a geranium-scented pound cake or pears sprinkled with a lemon-flavored herb accompanied by a mild cheese to help bring out the best in the beverage. Day-old toasted slices of geranium-scented pound cake are great for dipping, too.

If you are planning to serve these treats with a cup of herb tea, keep an eye on the herb's strength. An intensely robust (tart or spicy) herb tea, or one that's quite sweet, can be teamed with a mild-flavored dessert, but the reverse often doesn't work. Some experimenting and planning ahead of time can help you make the match.

The delicious finales collected here bring far more elegance to the table than their ease of preparation suggests. Some require several hours of cooling time, but none needs more than an hour of real attention. They are fast, easy, and delicious!

Christmas Day Dessert Buffet

Sparkling Apple Sangria

2   medium oranges
2   medium lemons
1/3 cup sugar
1   (6-ounce) can frozen apple
       juice concentrate, thawed
3   cups prepared Fredericksburg
       Texas Native Herb Tea, cooled
2   cups sparkling water

Juice 1 orange and 1 lemon. Mix juices and set aside. Cut remaining orange and lemon into thin slices. Place in a large pitcher. Sprinkle with sugar and crush with wooden spoon. Stir in reserved citrus juices, apple juice concentrate and prepared tea. Stir in sparkling water to taste. Pour into ice-filled glasses to serve.

Yields 8 servings

Floral Dessert Butter

Use fresh blossoms from plants such as roses, petunias, pansies, carnations, rosemary, thyme, oregano, or sage. Use only pesticide-free edible flowers.

    Fresh blossoms
1   pound unsalted butter, softened
3   tablespoons minced fresh mint
1/2 teaspoon lemon zest
1   tablespoon fruit preserves
1 1/2 teaspoons rose water
1   tablespoon chopped pecans

Rinse flowers thoroughly; pat dry between paper towels and set aside. Combine butter, mint, lemon zest, preserves, rose water and pecans in food processor container. Process until smooth and soft. Add petals from one blossom, processing until finely chopped and mixed with butter. Line bottom and side of wide-mouth 1-pint jar with petals from remaining blossoms, using butter to hold them in place. Fill jar with butter; place blossom on top. Chill, covered, for 3 days to allow butter to absorb flowers' flavor. Serve on bread, toast, muffins, bread-and-butter sandwiches or pancakes.

Yields 1 pound

Sparkling apple sangria

Floral dessert butter

Herb and butter
teddy bear bread

Cranberry cream cheese tart
with orange crust

Lemon balm cornucopia
cookies with minted berries and
lemon balm custard

Rosemary date nut pudding

Rose geranium pound cake

Sage-scented apples and prunes
with cinnamon dumplings

Herb and Butter Teddy Bear Bread

1   envelope dry yeast
1/8   teaspoon sugar
1/4   cup warm water
1/2   cup whipping cream,
        at room temperature
2   eggs, at room temperature
1   teaspoon salt
1   tablespoon fresh thyme
1   teaspoon fresh minced basil
1/2   cup sugar
1/2   cup unsalted butter, softened
4   cups flour
1   egg yolk
1   tablespoon milk

Sprinkle yeast and 1/8 teaspoon sugar over warm water in large bowl, stirring to dissolve. Let stand for 5 minutes or until foamy. Add cream, eggs, salt, thyme, basil and 1/2 cup sugar, mixing well. Stir in butter. Add flour 1/2 cup at a time, beating until soft dough forms. Knead on floured surface for 10 minutes or until dough is smooth and elastic, adding more flour as necessary. Place dough in large greased bowl, turning to coat surface. Let rise, covered, in warm place for 2 1/2 hours or until doubled in bulk. Punch down; knead on floured surface for 2 minutes. Divide dough into 2 equal portions. Place 1 portion in greased bowl, reserving it for second bear. Divide remaining dough into 2 equal portions. Roll 1 portion into a 3 1/2-inch ball. Place in center of parchment-lined baking sheet. Flatten dough to a 4 1/2-inch circle. Cut remaining portion into 2 equal pieces. Roll 1 portion into a ball. Place above circle on baking sheet and flatten to a 3 1/4-inch round to form the head. Pinch off a 1-inch round of remaining dough; place on center of head to form nose. Divide remaining dough into 6 portions. Roll each into a ball.

Attach 1 ball at each side of head, forming ears. Attach 1 ball at right and left of body, forming arms. Attach 2 balls, evenly spaced apart, on lower part of body to form legs. Pinch all edges to seal. Repeat process with remaining dough to form second bear. Let rise, covered, in warm place for 45 minutes or until doubled in bulk. Press fingertip into center of each ear to form indentation. Brush bears with mixture of egg yolk and milk. Bake at 400 degrees for 20 minutes; turn baking sheet. Bake for 20 to 30 minutes longer or until wooden pick inserted near center comes out clean. Remove to wire racks to cool. May be frozen for up to 2 months.

Yields 24 servings

Cranberry Cream Cheese Tart with Orange Crust

1 1/4 cups sugar

1   cup orange juice

3   cups fresh cranberries

1   teaspoon vanilla extract

10   ounces whole milk cottage cheese

6   ounces cream cheese, softened

2/3 cup sifted confectioners' sugar

3/4 teaspoon vanilla extract

1   (9 1/2-inch) deep-dish pie pastry

1   egg white

1   teaspoon water

4   teaspoons grated orange peel

2   tablespoons sugar

Combine 1 1/4 cups sugar and orange juice in saucepan. Bring to a boil, stirring until sugar dissolves. Boil for 1 minute longer. Add cranberries. Cook over high heat until berries pop and mixture resembles thick jam, stirring constantly. Stir in 1 teaspoon vanilla. Remove from heat to cool. Drain cottage cheese through fine sieve; set aside. Beat cream cheese in mixer bowl until light and fluffy. Add confectioners' sugar, 3/4 teaspoon vanilla and drained cottage cheese alternately, beating well after each addition until smooth. Chill, covered, until slightly firm. Press pie pastry into greased 11-inch springform pan. Brush with mixture of egg white and water. Sprinkle with mixture of orange peel and 2 tablespoons sugar, pressing lightly. Cover with foil and weight down with dried beans. Bake at 350 degrees for 12 minutes. Remove beans and foil. Bake for 5 to 10 minutes longer or until golden brown. Cool completely. Spread cranberry filling over crust. Chill for 30 minutes. Spread with cheese mixture. Garnish with fresh mint and grated orange peel. Chill for 30 minutes before serving. Garnish each slice with whole fresh cranberries.

Yields 8 servings

Lemon Balm Cornucopia Cookies with Minted Berries and Lemon Balm Custard

3 cups strawberries,
      cut into fourths
3 tablespoons sugar
1 1/2 tablespoons Grand Marnier
1 tablespoon minced fresh mint
1/4 cup sugar
2 tablespoons melted
      unsalted butter
1 teaspoon grated lemon peel
1 tablespoon minced fresh
      lemon balm
1 large egg white, at
      room temperature
1/4 cup flour
6 large egg yolks
6 tablespoons sugar
3 tablespoons whipping cream
4 1/2 tablespoons fresh lemon juice
6 tablespoons whipping cream
1 tablespoon minced fresh
      lemon balm

Sprinkle strawberries with 3 tablespoons sugar, Grand Marnier and mint in large bowl; stir gently. Chill for 2 to 4 hours. Process 1/4 cup sugar, butter, lemon peel and 1 tablespoon lemon balm in food processor until fluffy. Add egg white. Process for 2 to 4 seconds. Pour mixture into bowl; stir in flour. Spoon 1 tablespoon batter onto buttered baking sheet. Spread into a 5-inch circle. Repeat, having 2 circles on baking sheet at a time. Bake at 325 degrees for 12 minutes or until pale golden color. Loosen each cookie from baking sheet quickly; fold into cornucopia shape. Cool on wire rack. Repeat process until all batter is used. May prepare a day in advance and store in a single layer in an airtight container. Whisk egg yolks, 6 tablespoons sugar, 3 tablespoons whipping cream and lemon juice in double boiler. Cook over simmering water for 5 minutes or until mixture is thickened and no longer separates, stirring constantly. Pour into bowl to cool; press waxed paper on top to prevent skin from forming on custard. Beat 6 tablespoons whipping cream in mixer bowl until soft peaks form. Fold in 1 tablespoon lemon balm. Fold mixture into cooled custard. Fill cornucopia cookies with custard, allowing some custard to spill out onto dessert plate. Drain strawberries; spoon over custard. Garnish with fresh mint leaves.

Yields 8 servings

Rosemary Date Nut Pudding

1/4 cup shortening
1   cup sifted flour
1/2 cup sugar
1/2 teaspoon baking soda
1/2 teaspoon salt
1/3 cup buttermilk
1   egg
1   tablespoon grated orange peel
2   teaspoons minced fresh rosemary
1   cup finely chopped dates
1   cup coarsely chopped pecans
6   tablespoons Grand Marnier
2   tablespoons sugar
     Whipped cream
     Minced rosemary

Stir shortening in bowl to soften. Sift in flour, 1/2 cup sugar, baking soda and salt. Add buttermilk, egg, orange peel and 2 teaspoons rosemary. Beat for 1 minute or until smooth. Stir in dates and pecans. Spoon into greased 1 1/2-quart fluted high (cathedral) mold or 8 greased custard cups. Bake at 350 degrees for 25 to 30 minutes or until center tests done. Mix Grand Marnier with remaining 2 tablespoons sugar. Pour over hot pudding. Let stand for 15 minutes. Remove from mold or cups. Top with whipped cream; sprinkle with rosemary. Serve warm.

Yields 8 servings

Rose Geranium Pound Cake

6   rose geranium leaves
2 3/4 cups sugar
1   cup unsalted butter, softened
6   eggs
2   teaspoons rose water
1/2 teaspoon lemon extract
1   teaspoon vanilla extract
3   cups unbleached flour
1/4 teaspoon salt
1/4 teaspoon baking soda
1   cup sour cream
     Zest of 1 small lemon

Mince geranium leaves with sugar in food processor. Add butter. Process until light and fluffy. Add eggs 1 at a time, leaving processor running. Add rose water and lemon and vanilla flavorings. Sift flour, salt and baking soda together 3 times. Add alternately with sour cream to butter mixture, processing until smooth. Stir in lemon zest. Pour into greased and floured 10-inch tube pan. Bake at 300 degrees for 1 1/2 hours or until cake tests done. Loosen edge with knife; let stand in pan for 15 minutes. Invert onto wire rack to cool. Glaze or dust with confectioners' sugar.

Yields 12 servings

Sage-Scented Apples and Prunes with Cinnamon Dumplings

3/4 cup red zinfandel
3/4 cup water
1/2 cup sugar
12   jumbo pitted prunes
2   (1/4-inch) lemon slices
1 1/2 teaspoons minced fresh sage
3   medium McIntosh
     apples, sliced
1   cup flour
2   tablespoons sugar
1/2 teaspoon baking powder
1/4 teaspoon salt
1/2 teaspoon cinnamon
3   tablespoons chilled unsalted butter
2/3 cup milk
2   tablespoons sugar
1/2 teaspoon minced fresh sage

Christmas House Spray: A Seasonal Aroma for Your Home

Combine 4 drops of pine oil, 2 drops of orange oil, and 1 drop of cinnamon oil in a bowl.

Add 1 1/4 cups distilled water and mix well.

Pour into a spray bottle.

Bring zinfandel, water, 1/2 cup sugar, prunes, lemon slices and 1 1/2 teaspoons sage to a boil in heavy saucepan. Simmer and stir until sugar dissolves; reduce heat. Cook for 10 minutes. Add apples. Cook, covered, for 5 minutes or until apples are tender. Transfer fruit to 10-cup shallow baking dish, discarding lemon slices. Sift flour, 2 tablespoons sugar, baking powder, salt and cinnamon in bowl. Cut in butter until crumbly. Add milk, stirring just until moistened. Drizzle batter over fruit, using approximately 3 tablespoons per dumpling. Sprinkle with mixture of remaining 2 tablespoons sugar and 1/2 teaspoon sage. Bake at 425 degrees for 35 minutes or until dumplings are golden and syrup is bubbly. Spoon fruit and dumplings onto serving plates. Serve with cream. Garnish with small sage leaves.

Yields 4 to 6 servings

Holiday Good Scents

Special times are truly most memorable when associated with special aromas. Family traditions involving natural native materials have created the legacy that we enjoy today. Unfortunately, our urbanized lives have eliminated many natural products that gave us the original aromatic seasonal connection. Christmas pine trees have been coated with preservatives to stop their needles from dropping (inhibiting their scent, too) or have been replaced by silk trees. Wood fireplaces have given way to electric faux fires, poinsettias to plastic replicas, and fresh apple and pumpkin pies to flavorless,

heavily sweetened canned or premade varieties. Holidays just don't seem the same like that!

What smells do you associate with autumn, with Thanksgiving, with Christmas? Bayberry's aroma is popular. Traditionally, candles with this fragrance were burned in memory of the first settlers, who used the wax from the bayberry to make their candles. Today, candles still add a touch of warmth on cool days. To make a candle naturally aromatic, light it and wait until the wax begins to melt. Then add one drop of essential oil to it,

just by the wick. Bay, pine, and orange are joyous scents. Consider the following blend, too.

Fragrant Candle Blend

Cinnamon	1 drop
Geranium	1 drop
Orange	4 drops

The aroma of orange will evoke memories of holidays for all, while the geranium will put your guests in a good mood and the cinnamon will whet their appetites.

Does the resinous aroma of pine bring back memories of tree-trimming, decorating, Christmas lights, sweets, and gift-giving for you? If your tree isn't freshly cut, perk it up with a natural home spray. Spritz the tree with a mixture of 1 cup of water and 6 drops of essential oil of pine. Or, put a few drops of pine oil on a piece of absorbent material and tuck it around the base of the tree trunk. Many combinations of essential oils are evocative of special cozy times, too.

Spices	*Citrus*
Bay	Mandarin
Cinnamon	Orange
Clove	Tangerine
Trees	*Resins*
Cedarwood	Frankincense
Pine	Myrrh

The citrus oils are so fresh-smelling; they are our favorite choice to scent our home before visitors descend. Sweets containing the spice oils fill a home with the scent of personal hospitality. Try a drop of one or two of the following spice oils in your cooking: cinnamon, ginger, mace, nutmeg, clove, or cardamom. Use sparingly, only one drop per four ounces of ingredients.

What would entertaining be without decorations? Store-bought pine cones, corncobs, gourds, wreaths, and silk flowers are often dry and odorless. Help them come alive by putting them in a large plastic bag with a cotton wool ball that has absorbed several drops of essential oil. Seal the bag and leave it overnight. The next morning, your decorations will breathe a gentle fragrance, ready to create memorable good times.

With nature's essential oils, we have a special way of recreating the aromatic impact of old. But please, in using fragrances, do always aim to gently heighten the festive mood—not overpower its spirit!

The Working Garden

A Gardener's life, Is full of sweets and sours;
He gets the sunshine, When he needs the showers.
—Compensation, Reginald Arkell

"My Father is the husbandman."
—John 15:1

Pruning seems to be destroying the plant—the herb gardener appears to be cutting it all away! But, as with a child, the gardener looks into the future and knows that the final outcome will be the enrichment of its life and greater abundance of its harvest.

Continual trimming is the heart and soul of a Working Garden. In 1584, in the first English-language book on gardening, Thomas Hyll directed his readers to plant herbs in a straightforward, utilitarian layout: simple beds planted in narrow strips or squares of equal size. Each bed is enclosed with stone curbing or boarding; sides of the plot are sheared in hedge-like fashion for neat appearance; and young leaves are best for flavor. Both the tidy gardener and the cook are satisfied. "Threads of knots and mazes should be made with hyssop, thyme, lavender cotton, and other evergreen herbs which could be neatly clipped," wrote Hyll. How wonderful that these same hardy little herbs are still perfect—four centuries later—for a Working Garden.

We've placed most of the "how to, how often, how much" information in this chapter, along with a selection of entrées and side dishes. As a reward for all the hard work, we've also included a few desserts and some homemade ice creams.

Ready, Set, Plant!

In planning your garden, keep in mind those herbs which are easy to grow from seed, those which are more difficult, and those which are best started from plants.

Herbs That Come Readily from Seed

Anise	Fennel
Basil	Pennyroyal
(All varieties)	Rue
Borage	Saffron
Burnet	Sage
Caraway	Salad rocket
Chervil	(arugula)
Chives	Summer savory
Coriander	Sweet marjoram
(cilantro)	Thyme
Dill	

The following **herbs require patience** and, preferably, a spot where they will not disturb the rest of your garden while they take their time to appear and mature.

Balm	Mints
Catnip	Rosemary
Horehound	Winter savory
Hyssop	Woodruff
Lavender	Wormwood
Lovage	

The Following Herbs Should Be Started from Plants

Angelica	Santolinas
Artemisias	Scented geraniums
Germanders	Sweet Cicely
Mints	Tarragon
Rosemary	

When the few herbs you have acquired look straggly and lost, weak and pale, or overgrown and over-run, remember that it is almost impossible to produce a good garden in one or even two seasons. Don't get discouraged because of a few failures!

A Harvest Menu

Fredericksburg spiked
cranberry punch

Herbed tomato and
bleu cheese soup

Caraway scones with
flower petal butter

Anise apple pie

Fredericksburg Spiked Cranberry Punch

8   teaspoons (heaping)
    Fredericksburg Harvest
    Herb Tea
3   cups freshly boiled water
1/2 cup sugar
4   quarts chilled cranberry juice
1   (16-ounce) can whole
    cranberry sauce
2   cups vodka
1   (28-ounce) bottle tonic water
2   lemons, sliced

Place tea in warmed teapot. Pour
in water. Cover and let steep for
12 minutes. Strain tea, pressing
with back of spoon to extract all
possible liquid. Stir in sugar. Add
cranberry juice, cranberry sauce,
vodka and tonic water; mix well.
Add lemon slices and ice cubes.
Ladle into cups.

Yields 5 quarts

Herbed Tomato and Bleu Cheese Soup

1   tablespoon unsalted butter
1   onion, coarsely chopped
2   small cloves of garlic, minced
1   tablespoon flour
3   pounds ripe tomatoes,
    peeled, chopped
1   quart unsalted chicken stock
1   pound mild bleu cheese, crumbled
2   tablespoons tomato purée
8   fresh basil leaves, chopped,
    or 4 sprigs of dill, marjoram
    or oregano
    Salt and pepper to taste

Melt butter in large heavy
saucepan over medium-low heat.
Add onion and garlic. Cook until
garlic is translucent. Add flour.
Cook for 2 minutes, stirring
constantly. Add tomatoes, chicken
stock, cheese, tomato purée and
basil; mix well. Season with
salt and pepper. Bring to a boil;
reduce heat. Simmer for 2 hours
or until slightly thickened.

Yields 6 servings

Caraway Scones with Flower Petal Butter

1³/4 cups flour
1 teaspoon sugar
1 teaspoon salt
2 teaspoons baking powder
¹/2 teaspoon baking soda
2 teaspoons caraway seeds
5 tablespoons unsalted butter
³/4 cup (about) buttermilk
   Chopped freshly scented
      flower petals
   Butter

Combine flour, sugar, salt, baking powder, baking soda and caraway seeds in large bowl; mix well. Cut in 5 tablespoons butter until crumbly. Add enough buttermilk to make soft dough. Roll 1/2 inch thick on floured board. Cut into 1 1/2-inch rounds or cut with 2-inch cookie cutter. Place on ungreased baking sheet. Bake at 450 degrees for 10 to 12 minutes or until lightly browned. Mix flower petals with butter in bowl. Spread over scones. Good fall flowers to use include nasturtiums, pot marigolds, lavender, clover carnations, violets and borage.

Yields 12 scones

Anise Apple Pie

¹/2 teaspoon anise seeds
²/3 cup shortening
2 cups flour
¹/2 teaspoon baking powder
1 teaspoon salt
5 tablespoons cold water
¹/2 cup sugar
2 tablespoons flour
1 quart tart apples, peeled, sliced
¹/2 teaspoon anise seeds
¹/4 cup sugar
1 tablespoon lemon juice

Mix 1/2 teaspoon anise seeds with shortening in large bowl. Sift in 2 cups flour, baking powder and salt. Add water; mix well. Shape into a ball. Chill for 1 hour. Divide dough into 2 portions. Roll on floured surface. Fit 1 pastry into 9-inch pie plate. Sprinkle with mixture of 1/2 cup sugar and 2 tablespoons flour. Add apples. Sprinkle with remaining 1/2 teaspoon anise seeds, 1/4 cup sugar and lemon juice. Top with remaining pastry, fluting edge and cutting vents. Bake at 375 degrees for 50 minutes or until browned.

Yields 8 servings

"You cannot prevent the birds of sadness from passing over your head,
but you can prevent their making nests in your hair."
—Chinese Proverb

Texas Cooler Punch

11   cups cool water
8   teaspoons (heaping)
         Fredericksburg
         Texas Cooler Herb Tea
8   black tea bags
3/4 cup packed fresh mint leaves
1/2 cup honey
1/2 cup fresh lemon juice

Combine water, teas and mint in 3-quart or larger glass jar; cover. Let stand at room temperature for 12 hours or in sunny window for 6 hours. Strain mixture, pressing with spoon to extract all possible liquid. Heat 1 cup mixture with honey in small heavy saucepan. Cook until honey is melted, stirring constantly. Stir into remaining tea. Stir in lemon juice. Chill thoroughly. Pour into tall ice-filled glasses. Garnish with lemon slices and mint sprigs.

Yields 8 servings

Borage Cooler

12   borage leaves, minced
2   lemons, thinly sliced
1/4 cup sugar
4   cups water
4   cups sweet white wine (optional)
         Sprite or 7-Up to taste

Bring borage leaves, lemons, sugar and water to a boil in saucepan. Simmer for 20 minutes. Let stand to cool. Stir in wine. Chill thoroughly; strain. Serve over ice with a splash of Sprite or 7-Up. Garnish with borage flowers.

Yields 4 servings

How Much and How To's

When doubling a recipe, do not double the seasonings. Increase them by 1 1/2 times; then taste, adding more if desired.

How much of an herb should you use in cooking? The general rule is to use 1/4 to 1/2 teaspoon of dried herbs to four servings of food, and to use three times as much of the fresh herb as the dried. Taste, taste, taste!

The McCormick/Schilling Company tells us that "ground herbs and spices can be used in dishes with short cooking times while whole ones need a longer cooking time to release their

Don't let your clipped herbs die in the refrigerator!

Use them as decorative greenery for your table.

A bouquet of mint helps repel mosquitoes; a bouquet of parsley was once believed to ensure mealtime sobriety!

flavor." True—however, I've found that herbs (whether dried or fresh) produce the best flavor when half of them are reserved and added to soups and stews during the last fifteen minutes of cooking. (Garlic and bay are the exceptions.)

When combining herbs with steaming liquids, measure them away from the stove; rub them between your palms to release their flavor as you sprinkle them into the liquid.

Knock-Out Barbecue Baste

1/4 cup Fredericksburg
      Herbal Pepper Preserves
2   tablespoons soy sauce
1   tablespoon Fredericksburg
      Pepper Garlic Herb Vinegar
      or lemon juice
1   clove of garlic, minced

Combine preserves, soy sauce, vinegar and garlic in bowl; mix well. Use to baste poultry, fish or pork during last half hour of baking or last 10 minutes of grilling.

Yields 1/2 cup

Fresh Herb Marinade

1/2 cup melted butter
1/2 cup olive oil
2   tablespoons minced fresh dill,
      tarragon, rosemary, thyme,
      oregano, marjoram
      and/or basil
1   clove of garlic, minced
      Salt and freshly ground
      pepper to taste

Mix butter, oil, herbs and garlic in bowl. Brush generously over beef, fish, seafood, poultry or vegetables. Chill, covered, for 2 hours to overnight. Sprinkle with salt and pepper. Brush unused marinade over food while grilling.

Yields 3/4 cup or enough to marinate 3 pounds

Lemon Pepper Dry Rub

1/4 cup salt
1   tablespoon lemon pepper
1/2 teaspoon cayenne

Mix all ingredients in bowl. Use to season meat, poultry or seafood before barbecuing, roasting or broiling.

Yields heaping 1/4 cup

To Salt or Not to Salt

Salt will hardly be missed if you add an extra helping of savory to your cooking (summer savory for a mild piquant taste, winter savory for a peppery, heartier effect). Or sprinkle on minced dill, garlic, fresh ginger, an herb vinegar, or fresh lime or lemon juice to add the same sort of brightness that salt gives. When following recipes specifying salt, try eliminating the salt and add a quarter more of each herb than the amount called for.

Slow-Cooked Barbecued Beef Brisket

1   package Fredericksburg
       Herbs for the Grill
       Water or beer
1   (4-pound) beef brisket
       Lemon Pepper Dry Rub

Soak Herbs for the Grill in water or beer using package directions. Prepare barbecue grill by lighting fire at 1 end only. Rub brisket with dry rub. Sear brisket over white coals for 10 minutes, turning once. Move brisket to side of grill away from fire. Spread 2/3 of the herb mixture over the coals; cover grill. Smoke brisket for 1 hour at 200 degrees, sprinkling herb mixture with water occasionally. Spread remaining herb mixture over coals. Smoke for 1 hour longer. Wrap beef tightly in heavy-duty foil. Bake at 200 degrees for 8 hours. Slice thinly crossgrain. Serve hot.

Yields 4 to 6 servings

Parsley Pointers

If you can't grow your own, make dried herbs taste fresher by mincing them together with a fresh sprig of parsley; then add to your recipe. To keep purchased parsley perky, remove the rubber band, snip the tips off their stems, submerge them in a half inch of water in a glass, cover with a plastic bag, and store in the refrigerator. Recut the stems and change the water every few days. (Parsley is worth this extra care; it's full of vitamins A and C, thiamin, riboflavin, niacin, calcium, iron, magnesium, and phosphorous.)

Herbed Crown Pork Roast

1/4 cup Dijon mustard
1/4 cup margarine, softened
1 1/2 teaspoons rosemary
1 1/2 teaspoons thyme
1/4 teaspoon pepper
2 cloves of garlic, minced
1 (16-rib) crown roast of pork
1 cup beef broth
1 cup chicken broth
2 medium carrots, cut into pieces
2 stalks celery, cut into pieces
1 onion, cut into wedges
1/2 cup water
3 tablespoons cornstarch

Combine Dijon mustard, margarine, rosemary, thyme, pepper and garlic in bowl; mix well. Brush half the mixture on the roast. Place roast in roasting pan. Insert meat thermometer. Roast at 400 degrees for 20 minutes. Brush with remaining mustard mixture. Mix beef broth and chicken broth in bowl. Add 1 1/2 cups broth mixture, carrots, celery and onion to pan, reserving remaining broth mixture. Cover with foil. Reduce oven temperature to 325 degrees. Bake for 1 1/2 hours. Remove foil. Roast for 40 minutes longer or until meat thermometer registers 160 degrees. Place roast on heated serving platter. Discard vegetables. Pour drippings into cup. Let stand for several minutes; skim fat. Add enough reserved broth mixture to drippings to measure 2 1/2 cups. Return to roasting pan. Bring to a boil, stirring to deglaze pan. Stir water into cornstarch in bowl. Add to gravy. Cook until thickened, stirring constantly. Serve with roast.

Yields 16 servings

Herb-Roasted Turkey

1   (12-pound) turkey
6   sprigs of fresh thyme
4   sprigs of fresh rosemary
4   sprigs of fresh sage
$^1/_2$ teaspoon poultry seasoning
$^1/_4$ teaspoon salt
$^1/_4$ teaspoon pepper
1   medium onion, cut into quarters
2   stalks celery, cut into quarters

Rinse turkey inside and out, discarding neck, giblets and excess fat; pat turkey dry. Loosen skin carefully from breast and drumsticks. Arrange 1 thyme sprig beneath skin on each drumstick. Arrange 2 sprigs each of thyme, rosemary and sage beneath skin on breast. Mix poultry seasoning, salt and pepper together. Sprinkle into neck and body cavities. Place onion, celery and remaining thyme, rosemary and sage into cavities. Secure body cavity with skewers and truss turkey; tuck wings under back. Place breast side up on rack sprayed with nonstick cooking spray in shallow roasting pan. Spray turkey with cooking spray. Insert meat thermometer in meaty part of thigh, making sure it does not touch the bone. Cover loosely with foil. Roast at 325 degrees for 2 hours. Remove cover. Roast for 1 1/2 hours longer or until meat thermometer registers 185 degrees. Let stand, loosely covered, for 20 minutes. Place on serving plate. Garnish with parsley sprigs, orange sections and green and red grapes.

Yields 12 servings

Peach and Rosemary Chicken

6   chicken breasts
$1^1/_2$ cups peach preserves
$^1/_2$ cup Russian dressing
2   tablespoons freshly
      chopped rosemary
6   peach slices

Rinse chicken; pat dry. Place in baking dish. Spread with mixture of preserves and Russian dressing. Sprinkle with rosemary. Bake at 325 degrees for 45 to 60 minutes or until tender. Serve with peach slices. Garnish with rosemary sprigs.

Yields 6 servings

Roast Beef Tenderloin with Horseradish and Chive Sauce

2 (3-pound) beef tenderloin pieces
2 tablespoons crumbled
   dried rosemary
3 tablespoons cracked pepper
1/4 cup soy sauce
1/4 cup butter or margarine, softened
1 1/2 cups mayonnaise
1 1/2 cups sour cream or plain yogurt
1/3 cup chopped fresh chives
1/4 cup prepared horseradish
1/4 cup drained capers
   Freshly ground pepper to taste
   Ornamental kale

Rub beef with rosemary and cracked pepper. Let stand at room temperature for 2 hours. Preheat oven to 500 degrees. Brush beef with soy sauce; rub with butter. Place on rack in roasting pan. Insert meat thermometer into thickest portion of beef. Reduce oven temperature to 400 degrees. Roast beef for 40 minutes or until meat thermometer registers 120 degrees for rare. Chill beef in refrigerator. Combine mayonnaise, sour cream, chives, horseradish, capers and ground pepper in bowl; mix well. Spoon into serving bowl. Cut tenderloin into thin slices. Arrange on kale-lined serving plate. Serve chilled or at room temperature with sauce.

Yields 12 servings

Herb and Butter Rice

2 cups uncooked rice
6 tablespoons butter or margarine
2 tablespoons chopped fresh thyme
2 tablespoons chopped fresh basil
2 tablespoons chopped
   fresh tarragon
2 teaspoons chopped
   fresh rosemary
1/4 cup chopped fresh parsley
2 tablespoons chopped pimento

Cook rice using package directions. Add butter, herbs and pimento to hot rice; toss until butter melts and rice is coated. Spoon into serving dish.

Yields 8 servings

Seafood Gazpacho

1/4 cup chopped cucumber
1/4 cup chopped green bell pepper
1/4 cup chopped red bell pepper
1 tablespoon chopped
     jalapeño pepper
1/4 cup chopped red onion
1 1/4 cups chopped tomatoes
4 cups tomato juice
1/4 cup lime juice
3 tablespoons olive oil
1 cup fresh bread crumbs
1 teaspoon minced garlic
3/4 teaspoon cumin
     Salt and pepper to taste
4 ounces cooked shrimp
4 ounces cooked scallops
4 ounces cooked crab meat
1 small avocado, chopped

Combine cucumber, peppers, onion, tomatoes, tomato juice and lime juice in bowl; mix well. Stir in olive oil, bread crumbs, garlic and seasonings. Chill overnight. Add seafood; mix well. Ladle into soup bowls. Top with avocado.

Yields 8 servings

How Much Should Be Cut?

When harvesting perennial herbs, cut back one third, except for mints, sweet marjoram, chives, and oregano, which can be cut back to one inch above the ground.

Cut parsley, chervil, lovage, and caraway leaves to the ground at the edges of the plant, but leave the crown intact.

Cut dill and fennel back to their main stems.

Remember not to cut more than you can use.

Going to Pot

You may not be able to fool Mother Nature, but with some extra effort, she can be counterfeited. Outdoor facsimiles of soil, moisture, food, and light are the necessary components of surrogate parenting for an indoor herb gardener. Any container that will hold soil and that has adequate drainage holes—a clay pot, a hard plastic flowerpot, an empty plastic butter dish, a paint bucket—will usually work for an indoor environment. Even herbs that like moist soil do not want to be smothered by water! Clay pots are often preferred because of their natural look and because their porous walls allow soil to breathe. However, hard plastic flowerpots do not transpire moisture as readily as clay ones, so less frequent watering is needed.

More important than the type of container, though, is its size. Rosemary, for example, grows slowly, yet needs plenty of room— give it a 10-inch pot. Parsley needs a deep narrow pot to accommodate its long taproots—an 8- to 9-inch pot is adequate.

You must also consider the soil to be used. Individual herbs may prefer a rich or a sandy soil. Some like a very open soil so that very little moisture remains; others prefer greater moisture retention. Don't risk exposing your herb to disease spores or insect eggs by using questionable garden soil. Instead, use a sterilized potting soil, a soil-substitute mixture, or an equal combination of both, with sand or perlite for a light soil mix

or peat moss for a rich soil mix.

Too much water may be as bad for plants as too little. Tiny roots in waterlogged soil may die if they lack the air that is as necessary as water for their health. On the other hand, plants grown indoors in natural light during the winter may need more frequent watering to compensate for a dryer atmosphere. When you water your herb, soak the soil well and allow the water to drain thoroughly. Similarly, fertilizer over-feeding or under-feeding may cause plants to suffer. No feeding is recommended during low growth times—December, January, and February. Indoors, the greatest gardening problem is light—its quality will either slow growth or allow your herb to flourish. Aim for eight hours or more in natural light conditions.

Country Squash Casserole

1   pound yellow squash, sliced
8   ounces zucchini, sliced
1   cup water
1/2   cup chopped onion
1/4   cup chopped green bell pepper
3   tablespoons chopped green onions
1   tablespoon butter or margarine
1   cup herb-seasoned stuffing mix
3   tablespoons melted butter
      or margarine
1   (10-ounce) can
      cream of chicken soup
1   (8-ounce) can water chestnuts,
      drained, chopped
1/2   cup plain low-fat yogurt
1/4   cup chopped pimento
1   large carrot, grated
1/2   teaspoon salt
1/4   teaspoon pepper

Bring squash, zucchini and water to a boil in saucepan; cover and reduce heat. Simmer for 8 minutes

Bringing in the Sheaves Solution

After harvesting, cleaning, stripping leaves, and chopping herbs, my fingers show it.

They take on a beastly dark green-brown hue that can't be covered up or soaped off.

My beauty solution: Combine equal parts of lemon juice, vinegar, and water in a medium bowl.

Moisten your fingers in the lemon vinegar, rub them with salt, and rinse them in the lemon vinegar.

Repeat if necessary.

or until tender; drain. Sauté onion, green pepper and green onions in 1 tablespoon butter in skillet until tender; set aside. Mix stuffing mix with 3 tablespoons butter in large bowl; reserve 1/3 cup mixture for topping. Add squash mixture, sautéed mixture, soup, water chestnuts, yogurt, pimento, carrot, salt and pepper to remaining stuffing mixture; mix well. Spoon into lightly greased 8x12-inch baking dish. Sprinkle with reserved stuffing. Bake at 350 degrees for 30 minutes or until heated through.

Yields 8 servings

Broccoli with Orange Sauce

2   pounds fresh broccoli
2   tablespoons butter or margarine
2   tablespoons flour
1   cup orange juice
1   teaspoon grated orange peel
1/4   teaspoon tarragon
1/2   cup sour cream
1   cup orange sections

Trim broccoli; separate into spears. Cook in a small amount of water in saucepan for 10 minutes or until tender-crisp; drain. Melt butter in heavy saucepan over low heat. Blend in flour. Cook for 1 minute, stirring constantly. Add orange juice. Cook until thickened, stirring constantly. Stir in orange peel and tarragon; remove from heat. Stir in sour cream. Arrange broccoli on serving plate. Spoon sauce over top. Top with orange sections.

Yields 10 servings

Down Home Corn Pudding

1   (12-ounce) can whole
        kernel corn, drained
2   (17-ounce) cans
        cream-style corn
5   eggs, slightly beaten
1/2   cup sugar
1/4   cup cornstarch
1 1/2   teaspoons seasoned salt
1   tablespoon Fredericksburg
        Herbs de Provence Seasoning
1/2   teaspoon dry mustard
1   teaspoon onion flakes
1/2   cup milk
1/2   cup melted butter or margarine

Combine corn and eggs in large bowl; mix well. Mix sugar, cornstarch, seasoned salt, seasoning, dry mustard and onion flakes in medium bowl. Add to corn; mix well. Stir in milk and butter. Spoon into greased 3-quart baking dish. Bake at 400 degrees for 1 hour, stirring once.

Yields 8 servings

Sweet Potatoes in Apple Shells

6   large red baking apples
1   cup packed light brown sugar
5   cups mashed cooked
      sweet potatoes
1   tablespoon minced fresh sage
6   tablespoons melted butter
      or margarine
6   tablespoons whipping cream
2   tablespoons melted butter
      or margarine

Cut apples into halves lengthwise; core. Place in shallow baking dish. Sprinkle with half the brown sugar. Add a small amount of water. Bake at 400 degrees for 10 to 20 minutes or until slightly tender. Scoop out apple pulp, leaving 1/2-inch shells. Combine pulp, sweet potatoes, sage, 6 tablespoons butter and cream in mixer bowl. Beat until fluffy. Spoon into apple shells. Place in shallow baking dish. Sprinkle with remaining brown sugar. Drizzle with remaining 2 tablespoons butter. Bake at 400 degrees for 30 minutes or until heated through.

Yields 12 servings

Green Beans with Garlic

3   pounds young tender green beans
2   tablespoons extra-virgin olive oil
6   cloves of garlic, minced
$1/4$ cup dry bread crumbs
$1/4$ cup chopped flat-leaf parsley
      Salt and freshly ground
        pepper to taste
$1/4$ cup butter or margarine

Steam green beans for 6 to 8 minutes or until tender-crisp; drain. Refresh in ice water; drain. Heat olive oil in nonstick skillet over low heat. Add garlic, bread crumbs, parsley and seasonings. Cook for 1 minute, stirring constantly. Add butter. Cook until butter melts. Add green beans. Cook until heated through, stirring constantly. Arrange in serving dish.

Yields 12 servings

Mashed Potato Casserole

12   cups mashed cooked potatoes
8   ounces whipped cream cheese
2   eggs, beaten
1/4 cup finely chopped green onions
2   tablespoons finely
        chopped parsley
     Butter or margarine

Beat mashed potatoes with cream cheese in mixer bowl until smooth. Add eggs, green onions and parsley; mix well. Spoon into greased 1 1/2- to 2-quart baking dish. Dot with butter. Bake at 400 degrees for 30 minutes.

Yields 12 servings

Herb-Smoked Chicken

2   (2 1/2 -pound) chickens
     Lemon Pepper Dry Rub
1   package Fredericksburg
        Herbs for the Grill
     Water or sherry

Rinse chicken; pat dry. Rub chicken inside and out with dry rub. Wrap tightly in sealable plastic bags, removing all air. Chill for 24 hours. Soak Herbs for the Grill in water or sherry, using package directions. Mound coals on one side of barbecue and let burn to medium-low. Arrange chicken on grill rack away from coals. Mound 1 cup herb mixture over coals. Cook, covered, for 1 hour or until meat thermometer inserted in thigh registers 160 degrees, adding additional herb mixture if needed to maintain smoke. Remove chicken from grill. Bring coals to high heat. Grill chicken for 14 minutes or until skin is crisp, turning once.

Yields 6 to 8 servings

Marinated Vegetables

1   cup bite-size asparagus pieces
1   cup bite-size broccoli pieces
1   cup bite-size carrot pieces
1   cup bite-size summer
        squash pieces
3   cups Fresh Herb Marinade
     Finely minced chervil
        or parsley to taste

Boil or steam vegetables in unsalted water in saucepan until tender-crisp. Plunge into cold water; drain. Combine with Fresh Herb Marinade (page 83) in bowl; mix well. Chill overnight. Arrange on platter. Dust with chervil. You may add or substitute brussels sprouts, cauliflower, whole mushrooms and/or zucchini.

Yields 4 to 6 servings

Have You Tried?

Freezing Johnny-jump-
ups with distilled water in
ice cube trays?

Setting off an ice cream scoop
by placing it on a bed
of bright green rose leaves?

Substituting six tablespoons minced
white and yellow scented rose petals
for vanilla extract in cakes?

Steeping scented rose petals
in brandy (two weeks) for an
ice cream topping with bravo?

Joining the tips of two
separated nasturtium petals
with melted chocolate for a
"butterfly" garnish?

Lemon Verbena Peach Ice Cream

Pictured on page 95.

6   *rennet tablets*
¹/₄   cup cold water
2   *cups sugar*
¹/₄   cup fresh lemon verbena
4   *egg whites, beaten*
6   *cups milk*
6   *cups heavy cream*
4   *egg yolks, beaten*
2   *cups sliced peeled peaches*
4   *teaspoons vanilla extract*
    Peach slices
    Sprigs of lemon verbena

Crush rennet tablets in cold water to dissolve; set aside. Mince lemon verbena with sugar in food processor. Combine sugar mixture, egg whites, milk, cream, egg yolks, 2 cups peaches and vanilla in saucepan. Heat to 170 degrees, stirring constantly. Stir in rennet mixture. Pour into ice cream freezer container. Let stand for 10 to 20 minutes. Freeze using manufacturer's directions. Garnish each serving with a peach slice and a sprig of lemon verbena.

Yields 1 gallon

Lemon Verbena Peach Cobbler

This recipe is one of the biggest hits in our tea room! Many thanks to Jane E. Cook, who works in our tea room, for this addition.

4   *to 6 cups sliced peaches*
1   *cup sugar*
¹/₂   cup butter
¹/₄   cup sugar
2   *tablespoons lemon verbena*
    Zest of 1 lemon
1   *cup flour*
³/₄   cup sugar
1   *cup milk*
¹/₄   teaspoon salt
2   *teaspoons baking powder*
    Cinnamon to taste

Mix peaches with 1 cup sugar in bowl; set aside. Melt butter in 9x13-inch glass baking dish. Mince 1/4 cup sugar, lemon verbena and lemon zest in food processor. Combine flour, remaining 3/4 cup sugar, milk, salt and baking powder in large bowl; mix well. Stir in lemon verbena mixture. Pour over melted butter in prepared baking dish. Spoon peaches over batter. Sprinkle with cinnamon. Bake at 350 degrees for 1 hour or until bubbly and lightly browned.

Yields 10 to 12 servings

Lemon Pesto Pound Cakes

This recipe was contributed by Dee Lakari.

2   cups sugar
1   cup butter, softened
1/2   teaspoon baking soda
1/2   teaspoon baking powder
4   eggs
   Grated peel of 1 lemon
3   cups flour
1   cup buttermilk
1/2   teaspoon lemon extract
1/4   cup honey
1/2   cup walnuts
1/2   cup butter
2   tablespoons lemon juice
1/4   cup lemon basil leaves
1/4   cup cinnamon basil leaves
1/4   cup butter, softened
   Honey to taste

Cream sugar and 1 cup butter in mixer bowl until light and fluffy. Stir in baking soda and baking powder. Add eggs 1 at a time, beating well after each addition. Stir in lemon peel. Add flour and buttermilk alternately, beating well after each addition. Stir in lemon flavoring. Combine 1/4 cup honey, walnuts, 1/2 cup butter, lemon juice and basil leaves in food processor container. Process until mixed; reserve 2 to 3 tablespoons of this pesto mixture. Combine remaining pesto with 1/3 of the batter. Spoon remaining batter into 2 greased loaf pans. Swirl pesto batter into each. Bake at 350 degrees for 25 to 35 minutes or until loaves test done. Cut into slices. If you are using the cake as a tea bread, serve it warm. Mix reserved pesto with remaining 1/4 cup butter. Whip with a small amount of honey. Spread over warm tea bread slices.

Yields 16 to 20 servings

Vanilla Bean Chocolate Mint Ice Cream

Pictured on page 76.

6   rennet tablets
1/4   cup cold water
1   cup fresh chocolate mint
2   cups sugar
6   egg whites, beaten
6   cups milk
4   cups heavy cream
6   egg yolks, beaten
2   vanilla beans, split

Crush rennet tablets in cold water to dissolve; set aside. Mince mint with sugar in food processor. Combine sugar mixture, egg whites, milk, cream, egg yolks and vanilla beans in saucepan. Heat to 170 degrees, stirring constantly. Remove vanilla beans. Stir in rennet mixture. Pour into ice cream freezer container. Freeze using manufacturer's directions. Garnish each serving with a sprig of fresh chocolate mint.

Yields 1 gallon

Peach Brandy Pound Cake with Lemon Verbena

3   cups flour
1/4 teaspoon salt
4   (6-inch) sprigs of lemon verbena
3   cups sugar
1   cup butter, softened
6   eggs
1   cup sour cream
1   teaspoon orange extract
2   teaspoons rum extract
1/4 teaspoon almond extract
1/2 teaspoon lemon extract
1   teaspoon vanilla extract
1/2 cup peach brandy
1/2 cup baking cocoa
1/2 cup whipping cream
1/2 cup sugar
1/4 cup unsalted butter
2   tablespoons Cognac
1/2 cup peach jam

Mix flour together with salt. Mince verbena with 3 cups sugar in food processor. Cream 1 cup butter with sugar mixture in mixer bowl until light and fluffy. Add eggs 1 at a time. Add flour mixture and sour cream alternately to creamed mixture, beating well after each addition. Stir in flavorings and brandy. Spoon into greased and floured 10-inch bundt pan. Bake at 325 degrees for 1 hour or until cake tests done. Cool in pan for several minutes. Invert onto serving plate. Combine baking cocoa, whipping cream, 1/2 cup sugar and 1/4 cup butter in double boiler over simmering water. Cook until mixture is shiny and smooth. Cool for 5 minutes, stirring occasionally. Pour over cake, tilting cake to cover evenly. Spread icing over top and side of cake with thin flat spatula. Chill until icing is firm. Combine Cognac and jam in small heavy saucepan. Cook over medium-low heat until jam melts. Strain through fine sieve into small bowl. Cool to tepid. Pour over top of cake. Chill until glaze is set.

Yields 16 servings

Cinnamon Basil Ice Cream

6   rennet tablets
$^1/_4$ cup cold water
1   cup fresh cinnamon basil
2   cups sugar
6   egg whites, beaten
6   cups milk
4   cups heavy cream
6   egg yolks, beaten
$^1/_2$ tablespoon cinnamon
1   vanilla bean, split

Crush rennet tablets in cold water to dissolve; set aside. Mince 1 cup cinnamon basil with sugar in food processor. Combine sugar mixture, egg whites, milk, cream, egg yolks, cinnamon and vanilla bean in saucepan. Heat to 170 degrees, stirring constantly. Remove vanilla bean. Stir in rennet mixture. Pour into ice cream freezer container. Let stand for 10 to 20 minutes. Freeze using manufacturer's directions. Garnish each serving with a sprig of cinnamon basil.

Yields 1 gallon

Ginger-Mint Ice Cream

6   rennet tablets
$^1/_4$ cup cold water
2   cups sugar
6   egg whites, beaten
6   cups milk
4   cups heavy cream
6   egg yolks, beaten
2   tablespoons vanilla extract
$^1/_4$ cup chopped candied ginger
$^1/_2$ cup finely minced
        fresh peppermint

Crush rennet tablets in cold water to dissolve; set aside. Combine sugar, egg whites, milk, cream, egg yolks, vanilla, ginger and peppermint in saucepan. Cook over medium heat for 15 to 20 minutes or until heated through, stirring constantly. Stir in rennet mixture. Let stand for 10 minutes. Pour into ice cream freezer container. Freeze using manufacturer's directions.

Yields 1 gallon

Speaking of Herbs

Throughout the centuries flowers and herbs have signified a special language. In Elizabethan times the language of flowers was well-known; and small nosegays, or tussie-mussies, were given to convey lovers' messages. Victorian ladies perfected the art of sending floral messages as an acceptable way of circumventing social constraints. Planning specialized garden plots to grow the flowers and herbs for tussie-mussies was taken seriously. The herb gardens of churches were equally significant; during important festivals, churches were lovingly decorated with flowers and sweet-smelling herbs—draped over the altar, fastened to the walls, strewn on the floor, and even tied to the

sides of pews. Numerous legends sprang up to explain the meaning of the Christian saints' holy days and their herbs.

Consider a floral language revival of your own for an interesting way to plan your next holiday menu. A good meal beautifully presented cheers us. And one with the romantic and exotic touch of herbs feeds the soul as well as the body.

"Borage is for courage," according to the language of flowers. And indeed a garden without borage is like a heart without courage. When borage is grown among other plants, it is said to strengthen their resistance to disease and pests. I love its beautiful star-shaped blue flowers

and its hint of cucumber flavor. Our forefathers and foremothers candied the flowers, tossed them in salads, made sweet syrups of them, and floated them in wine cups to "make men and women glad and merry." Johnny-jump-ups, or hearts-ease, are equally beautiful and meaningful when used to garnish a glass of wine. Shakespeare knew them as "Cupid's flower," because they were thought to be the source of a powerful love charm. And aren't the holidays the perfect time to charm your loved one?

Mint carries a variety of connotations. It can communicate homey virtue, hospitality, wisdom, and cheer—all desirable sentiments, particularly when entertaining. Irish physicians of a hundred years ago said, "If you would be at all times merry, put a little mint in all your meat and drink." Perhaps the famous Kentucky mint julep derives from this background. A

"Seed catalogs are a triumph of hope over experience.
It's like having a second kid."
—Anonymous

sprig of mint in a holiday drink can quickly refresh guests, and it's also wonderful for the tummy after having overindulged! Whole leaves of salad burnet, a mild cucumber-flavored herb, were also once floated in cups of wine. Perhaps this accounts for burnet's sentiment of "a merry heart."

Parsley, the herb of festivity, is an important addition. In ancient Rome, parsley was used to honor victorious athletes. Wreathed chaplets of parsley were worn at Greek banquets to absorb wine fumes and prevent men from becoming inebriated. Today, this refreshing green can crown and enhance almost everything, as well as help to sweeten bad breath!

Basil can convey best wishes and love to welcome both old and new friends to your home. One legend says that eating basil rapidly develops a cheerful and merry heart (certainly a necessity when entertaining). An Italian legend held that a girl who gave her beau a sprig of basil was certain to win his affections; if he accepted her offering, he would love her forever.

Sweet marjoram's flavor is delicately spicy. Its sentiments of joy and happiness, of innocence and blushes, add a memorable touch of warmth to intimate gatherings. Wreaths of marjoram once crowned newly married couples to bring domestic peace. Another legend held marjoram to be the scent from the goddess Venus, who first planted it; her magic touch gave the herb its remarkable fragrance. Sage speaks of domestic virtue and happiness, too, as well as immortality and wisdom. As a preserver of youth, sage is believed to restore memory, clear the mind, and improve eyesight. It is a digestive and therefore of particular value to help survive a rich feast!

A holiday without rosemary for remembrance would definitely be incomplete. Rosemary is also an emblem for fidelity between friends and lovers. A home where rosemary flourishes supposedly signals that the woman rules. Rosemary invigorates the nervous system (it's certainly healthier than another cup of coffee) and may indeed strengthen the memory.

Taste pansy's center—its flavor is similar to root beer or cinnamon. Pansy's contribution to entertaining is primarily its bright color and texture. However, Ophelia in Shakespeare's *Hamlet* tells us, "Pansies—that's for thoughts."

We sincerely hope all your holiday entertaining will bring only the best of wishful thoughts from all those who enjoy your company.

Where to Put the "Early Bird" Herbs

(Not an all-inclusive list, but hopefully inspiring!)

Tirelessly making itself over, only a garden can surprise its guests with such wonders as a bulb just burst, or a hummingbird's unexpected visit to a new red bud. Fortunately, with some well-chosen herbal additions to our gardens, we can enjoy early signs of green and blooming life as spring returns.

For Part Shade	For Rock Gardens	For Ground Cover	For Containers
Bee balm	Burnet	Catmint	Alliums
Chamomile	Catmint	Chamomile	Chamomile
Chervil	Chamomile	Creeping thyme	Chives
Chives	Chives	Lady's mantle	Dittany
Comfrey	Costmary	Oregano	Lemon balm
Costmary	Dittany	Sweet woodruff	Oregano
Foxglove	Lady's mantle	Violet	Pansy
Lady's mantle	Pansy	Wild ginger	Parsley
Lemon balm	Parsley		Sage
Parsley	Thyme		Thyme
Sweet woodruff	Violet		
Thyme	Wild ginger		
Violet			
Wild ginger			
Yarrow			

Herbal Substitutions

If you're like me, you'll frequently not have on hand the herb specified in a dessert. The following substitutions are suggested, but I encourage you to try your own creative switches, too!

If the Recipe Calls For:	Try:
Anise seeds	Coriander, fennel, ginger, mint
Caraway seeds	Poppy seeds or sesame seeds, coriander
Fennel seeds	Anise seeds
Lemon balm	L. basil, L. geranium, L. thyme, L. verbena
Mint	Angelica, marjoram, L. thyme, rose geranium
Rosemary	Scented basil, bay, marjoram, L. thyme
Sage	Savory, thyme

The golden rule for setting out plants was always "after 4 p.m." and it is a practice well worth following. After this time, the sun's heat is decreasing in intensity and plants will have the benefit of "settling in" during the coolest part of the day.

Companion Planting

Even in the most ancient of times, gardeners claimed that many herbs are of great benefit when planted next to certain vegetables and herbs. On the other hand, some herbs are believed to hinder growth. Put into practice, the idea of companion planting may help in the garden by encouraging healthy growth, increasing flavor and fragrance, and repelling some pests and diseases. Listed below are (according to folklore) some helpful plantings and some that you may wish to avoid.

Plants That Help Each Other

Anise / Coriander

Basil / Vegetables,
    especially tomatoes

Borage / Strawberries

Caraway / Peas

Chamomile ("plant's physician") /
    Garden health

Chervil / Radishes

Chives (a natural pest repellent) /
    Leeks, carrots, apple trees

Dill / Cabbage, corn,
    lettuce, cucumber

Garlic, chives / Pest repellents
    for roses

Horseradish / Potatoes, fruit trees

Hyssop / Grapes

Lavender, thyme / Vegetables

Lovage / Potatoes, root vegetables

Mint / Rosemary / Sage

Nasturtium / Apples

Parsley / Tomatoes, roses

Rosemary, sage / Carrots

Sage / Cabbage

Salad burnet / Thyme / Mint

Sorrel / Oregano

Southernwood / Cabbage

Summer savory / Onions

Thyme / A natural pest repellent

Winter and summer savory / Beans

Yarrow / Increases fragrance
    of most herbs

Plants That Suppress Each Other

Basil / Rue

Caraway / Fennel

Chamomile / Peppermint

Coriander / Beans, tomatoes

Dill / Carrots

Fennel / Beans, tomatoes

Garlic, chives, leeks, shallots /
    Beans, peas

Hyssop / Carrots, radishes

Wormwood / Plant off in a corner

Indoor Pot Planting Guide
(from John Brimer's Growing Herbs in Pots)

Herb	Soil	Water	Food	Sun	Replant	Pot Size
Basil	A,RI	W,C	M,F	S/PS	Y	8"
Chives	RI	W,G	M,H	S	K	6"
Dill	A,RI	W,G	M	S	Y	6"
Marjoram/ Oregano	A,L	W,C	M,H	S	Y	8"
Mint	B,RI	W,C	M,F	PS/S	Y,K	12"
Parsley	A,RI	W,C	M,H	S/PS	Y	8"
Rosemary	A,L	W,C	M,F	S/PS	RE-4 to 5	10"
Sage	A,L	W,G	M,F	S	RE-3 to 4	8"
Tarragon	A	W,D	M,H	S	Y,K	12"
Thyme	RI,L	W,D	M,H	S	RE-2 to 3	8"

KEY:

Soil: A Average B Humusy L Light RI Rich

Water: W Weekly C Moist G Barely moist D Dry

Food: M Monthly F Full-strength H Half-strength

Sun: S Full sun PS Partial sun

Replant: Y Yearly K Divide RE Replace, number of years

Aromatherapy for the Garden

In the plant world, aroma can be a matter of life and breath. Isn't reproduction, "the birds and the bees," all about pollen wafted from one plant to another? Aroma is critical: Highly scented flowers tend to be fertilized by butterflies and moths, fruity aromas attract beetles, and plants with nasty, fishy smells attract dung-flies and flesh-flies. Aroma, however, may protect a plant, too, by making it repugnant or poisonous to certain insects and larger animals.

Buggy Blooms?

They hide in all the nooks and crannies of your fresh-picked flowers, only to make their presence known at the dining room table when you're ready to serve that beautiful petal-topped salad!

To flush out those nasty bugs, briefly soak the flowers in a bath of vinegar and cold water.

Use approximately one tablespoon of vinegar to one cup of water.

Rather than spraying pesticides or herbicides or trapping armadillos, we suggest trying natural essential oils or growing naturally repellent plants in your garden to help control pestiferous critters. Some gardeners claim that using essential oils or growing certain plants will even make your flowers, herbs, fruits, and vegetables stronger, better tasting, and more fragrant. Along with being safer, we hope, they will make your own time in the garden altogether more enjoyable. Here is a brief list of some common pests and their dislikes.

Insect	Repellent Plant	Essential Oil
Ants	Spearmint, tansy, pennyroyal, peppermint *Grow plants near doors of house, in pots or ground.*	Spearmint, peppermint, pennyroyal, garlic, citronella *Put oil on cotton balls, place by doors. Spray oils along shelves where ants are seen, and on their nests.*
Aphids	Nasturtium, spearmint, stinging nettle, southernwood, garlic, potatoes, parsley, basil, horseradish	Spearmint, peppermint, cedarwood, hyssop
Black flies	Stinging nettle, basil, lavender	Lavender, tansy
Caterpillars	Celery, tomatoes	Spearmint, pennyroyal, peppermint
Fleas	Lavender, mint	Lemongrass, citronella, pennyroyal, rue, tansy, lavender, eucalyptus
Flies	Rue, tansy, wormwood, tomatoes *Rue is especially helpful grown around composts and barns.*	Rue, lavender, citronella, peppermint, tansy
Gnats	Pennyroyal	Citronella, patchouli, spearmint
Mosquitoes	Sassafras, pennyroyal, wormwood, southernwood, rosemary, sage, santolina, lavender, mint	Lavender, pennyroyal, sassafras, citronella, lemongrass, tansy
Moths	Wormwood, southernwood, rosemary, sage, santolina, lavender, mint, tansy	Spearmint, lavender, hyssop, citronella, peppermint
Slugs	Garlic, chives, wormwood	Garlic, cedarwood, hyssop, sassafras, pine
Snails	Garlic	Cedarwood, sassafras, pine, garlic, patchouli
Weevils	Garlic	Cedarwood, rue, sandalwood, patchouli
Wooly aphids	Nasturtium	Sandalwood, patchouli, pine

The Star Garden

See how the flowers, as at parade, Under their colours stand displayed:
Each regiment in order grows, That of tulip, pink and rose.
—Andrew Marvel (1621–1678), "The Garden"

A Stellar Herbal Display

Planted in the shape of a star and centered around an antique windmill, the largest of Fredericksburg Herb Farm's gardens measures approximately 180 feet in diameter—and many hours in toil. Each of the five star points is devoted to a single theme: culinary herbs, medicinal herbs, herbs of a certain color, flowers and herbs suitable for crafts, and herbs essential to cosmetics.

Considered by some friends to be a star for the Republic of Texas, by others to be an Egyptian hieroglyphic signifying "rising upwards" or "to educate," and by others to be a symbol of the manifestation of Christ to the Gentiles, the Star Garden is an herbal heaven.

In this chapter, there is information about two wonderful herbs—rosemary and thyme—complete with recipes. We also show how you can make your own vinegars and dressings and how to preserve herbs and flowers. There are cosmetic and medicinal uses for herbs—and even an edible present for your pet.

"Observe your dog: if he's fat you're not getting enough exercise."
—Evan Esar

Dog and Cat Biscuits

2   tablespoons margarine, lard
      or bacon fat, softened
1   teaspoon brown sugar
1   egg, slightly beaten
1/2 cup dry milk powder
1/2 cup chicken broth
1   cup all-purpose flour
1   cup whole wheat flour
1/2 cup wheat germ
1/2 teaspoon salt
1/2 cup catnip (for cat biscuits)
8   large cloves of garlic,
      crushed (for dog biscuits)

Cream margarine and brown
sugar in mixer bowl until light

and fluffy. Beat in egg, dry milk
and broth. Add flours, wheat
germ and salt; knead until soft
dough forms. Shape into a ball.

Let stand, covered, for 30
minutes. Roll 1/4 inch thick on
lightly floured surface. Sprinkle
with catnip or garlic; pat lightly
into dough. Cut with 3-inch fish-
shaped or bone-shaped cookie
cutter. Place on lightly greased
baking sheet. Bake at 325
degrees for 30 minutes or until
browned and crisp. Cool on wire
rack. Store in airtight containers.

Yields 3 dozen

For many friends, an animal is the constant and comforting presence in their lives.
Make sure the pet gets an edible present early for special occasions—or for no-reason-at-all moments.

An Herb Ahead of Its Time

Remember, man was once completely dependent on the garden for medicine, food, and flavor! Many centuries before refrigeration, the appeal of rosemary was utilitarian. Nature was the vital force behind new ideas; people became convinced that since wrapping meats in crushed rosemary preserved the food (as well as imparted a delicious fragrance and flavor), a similar preservative effect would be possible on the human mind and spirit.

Greek students would twine rosemary in their hair to fortify and refresh the brain at exam time. Garlands were also worn to ward off the "evil eye." Taking on the personality of remembrance, the herb grew into an emblem of love.

An uprooted Mediterranean native, rosemary arrived in Britain with the Roman armies. Centuries passed; rosemary wove its way into weddings to assure spousal fidelity, into funerals as a memorial for those deceased. During the Middle Ages, rosemary was endowed with a charmed quality: If a young person tapped another with a rosemary twig bearing an open blossom, the couple would fall in love. Placed under a pillow, the aromatic herb repelled all evil dreams. Planted around a home, it was reputed to ward off witches. In sixteenth century England, a flourishing rosemary plant signified a household where the woman ruled. Men were known to rip out rosemary plants as evidence that they—and not their wives—ruled the roost!

Rosemary's utility continued to flourish, though: Culpeper maintained that "to burn the herb in houses and chambers, correcteth the air in them." It was the Lysol of its day—used as a strewing herb, it cleansed the air in drafty, smoky castles. Clothes and bed linens were stored in chests filled with it. Little cakes or drops made of the flowers and sugar were supposed to comfort the heart and quicken the spirits. The flowers alone were eaten "to procure a clear sight"; the powder made of the flower dusted many a man's body in hopes of making him "merry, glad, gracious and well-beloved of all men"—and of all the fairer sex, too! Tossed on the fire, rosemary was the flavor of choice for a spit-turned leg of lamb.

In fact, meats may be preserved by rosemary. Meats spoil in part because their fats oxidize and turn rancid. Rosemary and its compound essential oil, rosmaricine, contain chemicals that are strongly antioxidant.

Like discovering the fountain of youth, research attributes to rosemary stimulation of the circulatory, digestive, and nervous systems. Rosemary is an herb with promise for relief from headaches, indigestion, depression, muscle pain, bad breath (used as a gargle), and premature baldness (as an external hair rinse). Abundant in calcium (a mineral known to calm nerves), rosemary in the bathtub "takes you away" from stress, replenishing your psychic energy and leaving you with an oceanic freshness.

Sweet Rosemary Grape Pickles

These pickles are delicious with meats, poultry, fish, and cheeses.

2   pounds seedless white grapes
1   pound raw sugar
$^1/_2$ cup distilled white vinegar
2   teaspoons mustard seeds
$^1/_2$ teaspoon cinnamon
$^1/_2$ teaspoon allspice
$^1/_2$ teaspoon cloves
$^1/_2$ teaspoon nutmeg
3   (4-inch) sprigs of fresh rosemary
$1^3/_4$ ounces powdered fruit pectin

Wash grapes in cold water; remove stems. Combine sugar and vinegar in large saucepan. Stir in spices and herbs. Bring to a boil. Simmer for 15 minutes, stirring occasionally. Remove rosemary sprigs. Add grapes; sprinkle in pectin. Return to a boil; simmer for 3 minutes or until syrupy. Skim off foam, stirring occasionally; remove from heat. Let stand for 10 minutes. Spoon into hot sterilized jars, leaving a 1/2-inch headspace; seal with 2-piece lids. Use within 4 weeks.

Yields 2 pints

The Star Garden

"Grow young along with me! The best is yet to be. The last of life, for which the first was made."
—Browning

Rosemary Tea

This recipe comes from Judith Benn Hurley's *The Good Herb*. Breathe deeply while sipping this warm tea to inhale the aromatic steam and boost the tea's calming effect.

2   tablespoons fresh rosemary
      or 1 tablespoon dried
1   cup boiling water
      Lemon or orange twist
      Honey to taste

Place rosemary in sturdy mug. Pound rosemary lightly with spoon to release aroma. Pour in boiling water. Steep, covered, for 4 minutes; strain. Add lemon or orange twist and honey to remove strong, piny taste.

Yields 1 cup

Robert Browning musing on the herb rosemary?

We suggest that the gloomiest, darkest days in winter are the best time to appreciate an herb that "will keepe thee youngly," according to one herbal.

Glorious rosemary! It looks like a diminutive woody tree with pine-needle-like leaves, dark green above and white beneath.

The leaves taste pine fresh, with a hint of pepper that leaves a warm feeling within.

In the axils of the leaves pink, blue, or white flowers bloom— similar to tiny orchids.

Rosemary Walnuts

1/4   cup cold unsalted butter,
        cut into 4 pieces
2   tablespoons very finely
        minced rosemary
1/4   teaspoon salt
1/8   teaspoon cayenne
2   cups walnut halves

Combine butter, rosemary, salt and cayenne in foil-lined jelly roll pan. Bake at 400 degrees until butter melts; remove from oven. Add walnuts; toss to coat. Bake for 6 to 9 minutes or until walnuts are lightly toasted, stirring at 3-minute intervals. Cool slightly before serving. Store in airtight container.

Yields 2 cups

Rosemary Know-How

❧ Rosemary's pine-camphor-citrus aroma comes from five main volatile oils and no fewer than eighteen minor ones—hard to pair with other herbs. Garlic and onion are exceptions; they're robust but not combative. Lavender also works with rosemary since it contains some of the same volatile oils.

❧ Use two teaspoons of minced fresh leaf in a recipe to serve four. If you have only dried rosemary, use a teaspoon in a recipe to serve four. (Dried leaves are tough little spikes! Finely mince for comfortable chewing.)

❧ Tradition combines rosemary with heavy food—lamb and duck—because its piercing pine flavor really cuts the fat.

❧ Rosemary also enhances lighter food—winter squash, baby new potatoes, green beans, and dried beans, as well as balsamic vinegar-based marinades and vinaigrette.

❧ Top this! Flavor a pizza with chopped rosemary, sliced tomatoes, grilled onions, and cheese.

❧ Lunch box extraordinaire! Try grilled rosemary and goat cheese sandwiches on pumpernickel or rye bread.

❧ Add 1 tablespoon chopped fresh rosemary to a favorite corn muffin or biscuit recipe.

❧ Knead chopped fresh rosemary into hearty wheat, rye, or whole grain dough for savory breads.

❧ Make an herbed butter by blending 1 tablespoon each of chopped fresh rosemary, sage, thyme, and parsley with 1 cup softened unsalted butter.

❧ Prevent food poisoning on your next picnic: Mix crushed rosemary leaves generously into hamburger meat, tuna, pasta, or potato salads.

❧ For rosemary wine, steep 1 cup fresh trimmings in a fifth of good quality claret, rosé, or white wine.

❧ Tie a couple of sprigs of rosemary together with some raffia to make an herbal whisk. Send it along with a thank-you note for a recent dinner party because "Rosemary is for remembrance."

Potting Mix for Rosemary

Indoors, big pots of rosemary reach for filtered southern sun, a six-hour sustenance. They prosper in a cool spot (45 to 55 degrees). For plants that have been growing without pots, dig deeply around the circumference of their leaf or branch spread; then lift the plant gently from the ground. At this point, it's easy to tell what size pot they'll need.

Rosemary likes well-drained soil, a bit gritty and slightly alkaline. The standard herb soil mixes two parts garden soil or potting soil, two parts peat, one part sand, and one part compost or composted cow manure. (Work a few eggshells into the sand-perlite mix when potting up rosemaries for the house.) Put the plant in the clay pot, firm up the soil around the root ball, and feed with a dilute solution of fish emulsion. Place potted rosemaries on a tray of pebbles; this prevents water from sitting in the pots and provides some added moisture to the area where the plants are growing. Water only when the soil is dry; dig a finger into the soil—if it is almost dry, give it a drink. Feed lightly once a month with diluted fish emulsion. Fried green rosemary? If the room heats up during the day, please do water-spritz the leaves!

Asparagus Bundles with Thyme Blossom Butter

$1^1/_2$	pounds fresh asparagus, trimmed
8	scallion stems
2	tablespoons butter, softened
2	tablespoons grated lemon peel
2	tablespoons fresh lemon juice
$^1/_2$	cup thyme blossoms

Steam asparagus and scallion stems in a small amount of water in saucepan until tender-crisp; drain. Arrange asparagus stalks into 4 bundles; tie bundles with scallion stems. Place bundles on serving plate. Combine butter, lemon peel, lemon juice and half the thyme blossoms in bowl; mix well. Spoon onto asparagus bundles. Garnish with remaining 1/4 cup thyme blossoms.

Yields 4 servings

I know a bank whereon the wild thyme blows.
—Shakespeare, A Midsummer Night's Dream

What Thyme Do You Have?

One of the strongest of seasoning plants, all thymes are meant to be used with a light hand. Thyme will add a soft, plummy fragrance and subtle taste compounded of mint, bay, and marjoram to almost any cooked food: rice, meats, eggs, most vegetables (especially potatoes, carrots, tomatoes), and fish.

Thymes are easily grown from seed. Sow the tiny round seeds on moist soil; cover with a very fine layer of sifted soil. Keep the soil evenly moist. You should see seedlings emerge after seven to fourteen days at 70 degrees. You can begin transplanting to individual pots after the second

set of true leaves appears. In the garden, thymes thrive (and are most flavorful) when given lots of sun—an absolute minimum of four hours. They also need good, well-drained soil, ideally a sandy loam. Thymes grow happily in containers indoors, or outdoors, as long as their basic needs for sun and good drainage are met.

Our shop offers four to start from seed: creeping, English, French, and garden thyme. Although many thymes are similar in their sweetish, delicately pungent, pepper-green herb aroma, these thymes are distinctive in their growing habits and in their miniature leaf size and color.

Thymes' shrublet varieties— English, French, and garden— grow close to the earth, eight to twelve inches in height, on one or more woody trunks. Side branches grow upward, usually supporting themselves, forming plump mounds thick with tiny leaves and white

to rosy-lavender fairy-size flowers.

Garden, or common, thyme, *T. vulgaris*, is the thyme of choice for cooking or drying. It is the easiest of the shrubby forms to cut and the easiest to gather in any quantity.

English, or broad-leaf, thyme is darker green with wider, more oval leaves. In food, English thyme has more mint undertones than the garden or French; it is particularly good in hearty meat dishes and on grilled vegetables. French, or narrow-leaf, thyme has decurved, grayish-green leaves. Its flavor is the subtlest of the thymes. It goes well in a bouquet garni and deepens in flavor in a long-cooked soup or stew.

Creeping thyme, or mother-of-thyme, *t. serpyllum*, grows barely a few inches tall; it is perfect for the inter-spaces of flagstone paving, banks, rock gardens, and raised beds in herb gardens. Although it is not particularly useful in the kitchen, its red-purplish flowers provide a magic carpet for hummingbirds, children, and bees. The soft floppy branches spread quickly along the ground, forming a thick ground cover, and usually rooting along the entire length of its branches. Our dream, though, of our farm's creek bank covered in thyme, will take years to realize. Weeding out all other plants so that the divisions will have a chance to spread over a large area is a time-consuming and patience-trying process.

Some final advice—because thyme is so hardy, a plant may thrive for years. When thyme is grown for culinary use, we suggest that it be replaced every two to three years, or pruned sharply each spring, to ensure good fragrance on young, supple stems.

Many other exciting varieties of thyme—lemon, caraway, wooly—cannot be grown from seed, because they do not produce both male and female flowers necessary for self-pollination. However, all varieties of thyme are usually available in two-inch to four-inch pots.

Thyme and Rice Pilaf

1   cup long grain rice
2   tablespoons cooking oil
2   cups chicken stock
3   tablespoons fresh thyme

Sauté rice in oil in saucepan over medium heat until golden brown, stirring constantly to avoid burning. Add chicken stock and thyme. Simmer, covered, for 15 to 20 minutes. Fluff with fork; serve hot.

Yields 3 to 4 servings

A Note About Our Herbal Vinegars

Only organically grown, freshly harvested herbs and flowers from Fredericksburg Herb Farm's fields are selected to create our herb vinegars. Our Basil Blush, Pepper-Garlic, Lovely Lemon, Scarborough Fair, and Edible Flower vinegars are free of sugar, salt, additives, and preservatives. A splash of our vinegar has the essential elements—freshness, earthiness, sweetness, and tartness—to turn simple food into cuisine that is elegant and satisfying.

Our philosophy about making and enjoying herbal vinegars is quite simple: We want as much fresh-picked garden flavor and natural artistry as possible. Consequently, each etched-glass bottle is carefully formulated to assure its unique character and beauty; we hand-pack the choicest garnishes and hand-pour the wine vinegar aged with herbs and flowers.

Our herbal vinegars can be substituted in almost any recipe that calls for plain vinegar and can be used just as you would lemon or lime juice to enhance food. Here are a few suggestions.

A splash over cooked vegetables renews some of the fresh-picked flavor lost in commercial vegetables.

Use them to perk up vinaigrettes for raw vegetables. Our favorite is a simple cucumber and red onion marinade.

To enhance flavor and tenderness, add our vinegars while marinating and basting seafood, poultry, or meat as it grills or roasts. This will balance the richness of the meat and help to counteract greasiness.

Try substituting our vinegars for lemon juice in salad dressing, dips, sauces, and Bloody Mary cocktails for unique sparkle and spice.

Vinegar Lesson

Vinegars have a reputation of being sour, cider-tasting, plastic-bottled liquids, to be sparingly sprinkled on salads as an afterthought for the diet-conscious. The first vinegar may well have been an accident—perhaps someone left the wine out in the hot sun. It "turned" and became vinegar. "Vinegar" comes from a medieval French term, "vin aigre," or sour wine. The first herb vinegar, too, may have been a mistake—a cook throwing a handful of herbs to cover up some wine-gone-sour, forgetfully putting it aside.

Since that time, herb vinegars have been put to culinary, medicinal, and even cosmetic use.

Recipe for Herbal Incense

After drying leaves
of lemon verbena, rosemary,
scented geraniums,
or lavender, separately
rub each herb through
a fine sieve, then store in
individual bottles.

To clear the air of unpleasant
odors, place a handful of
the leaves in a votive candle
holder and light the mound.

Wine vinegars are made from all types of wine from many different countries. Balsamic vinegar is considered to be the ultimate. Made in Modena, Italy, since the sixteenth century, balsamic vinegar was so valued that it was often included in a bride's dowry or in a family inheritance. Dark, rich, sweet, and pungent, balsamic vinegar is the fermented juice of Trebbiano grapes. As with old Cognac, wooden vats of oak, walnut, or cherry store the vinegar until maturity—traditionally, ten years.

Making Your Own Herb Vinegars

Homemade vinegars make great gifts and are beautiful displayed in your own kitchen, as well. If made correctly, these vinegars will last for years. Give it a try! Consider using any of the following herbs in your vinegars: basils—lemon, cinnamon, sweet, lettuce leaf, purple ruffled, Italian; bay leaves, chervil, chives, cilantro, dill, fennel, French tarragon, garlic, lemon balm, lemongrass, lemon verbena, lovage, marjoram, Mexican mint marigold, mints, oregano, parsley, rosemary, sage, savory, scented geraniums; thymes—English, French, lemon.

It is best to harvest herbs in the morning when the herbs are freshest and have the most flavor. Clean them, making sure no bugs are hiding within.

Fill a clean, sterilized glass bottle or jar with the fresh herbs.

We suggest using 2/3 white vinegar to 1/3 white or red wine to make your vinegar more mellow; this takes the bite or sharpness out. Pour the vinegar/wine mixture over the herbs; bruise the herbs with a wooden spoon.

Cover the container and store in a cool, dark place at room temperature. Stir the mixture once every four or five days with a wooden spoon. Your vinegar should be ready in three to six weeks, depending upon how strong you wish the vinegar to be.

Filter/strain the herbs from the vinegar. (A coffee filter and a funnel work fine!)

Place a few clean, fresh herb sprigs in a clean, attractive bottle.

Pour the vinegar over the sprigs. Label and enjoy!

Here are a few herb combinations you can use to make an unusual bottle of herb vinegar. Be creative and have fun!

Basic Herb Vinegar

$1/2$ cup sweet basil
$1/2$ cup rosemary
$1/4$ cup Mexican mint marigold
4   bay leaves
$1/4$ cup oregano
1   teaspoon mixed peppercorns
1   teaspoon whole cloves

Follow the basic directions given above.

Hill Country Peaches and Herb Vinegar

2   cups peaches, cleaned, peeled
1   cup fresh cinnamon basil
2   long cinnamon sticks

Follow the basic directions given on page 121.

Olé Herb Vinegar

1½ cups assorted peppers
1   cup fresh cilantro
2   cloves of garlic
1   or 2 green onions
3   or 4 sprigs of thyme

Follow the basic directions given on page 121.

Marinade of Simples

Herbs were once called "simples" by the Shakers, who grew and gathered them for their homes.

To make your own simple, combine ½ cup oil; ¼ cup vinegar, wine, or lemon juice; 1 crushed garlic clove; ¼ cup chopped chives; ¼ cup chopped parsley; and 1 tablespoon each minced fresh basil and fresh rosemary.

Soak meat, poultry, or vegetables for at least one hour before grilling.

Festive Herb and Edible Flowers Vinegar

1   cup chives
½ cup dill
1   cup mint
½ cup fennel

Follow the basic directions given on page 121. When doing your final bottling, put in freshly cleaned blossoms from chives, dill, borage, lavender, and mint.

Boosting Flavors with Vinegar

Use Basil Blush, Scarborough Fair, or Pepper Garlic Herb Vinegar in place of one-fourth of the liquid in preparing dry sauce mixes, such as spaghetti, taco, and gravy.

After sautéing meat, pour a few tablespoons of Classic Herb, Scarborough Fair, or Pepper Garlic Herb Vinegar into the pan and combine it with any browned particles left from the meat to make a quick savory sauce.

Add 1 tablespoon Lovely Lemon, Edible Flowers, or Basil Blush Herb Vinegar to cake batter, cookie dough, puddings, or pie fillings to add moisture and lightness.

Use Classic Herb, Edible Flowers, Pepper Garlic, or Scarborough Fair Vinegar as part of the liquid (one spoonful per serving) in preparing a favorite soup or stew.

Splash Edible Flowers or Mediterranean Balsamic Vinegar on sweetened fresh or frozen fruit.

Substitute Basil Blush, Lovely Lemon, or Edible Flowers Herb Vinegar for part of the fruit juice in jelly recipes that include pectin.

Ginger and Lime Dressing for Fruit

2	tablespoons minced fresh ginger
1	tablespoon sugar
1/4	cup honey
	Juice of 4 limes
	Juice of 4 lemons
1/4	cup Fredericksburg Olive Oil

Combine ginger, sugar, honey and juices in small saucepan. Bring to a boil, stirring constantly; reduce heat. Simmer for 3 minutes. Cool to room temperature. Whisk in olive oil. Pour over favorite fruit plate.

Yields 1 cup

Honey Flower Dressing

$^1/_3$ cup Fredericksburg
    Edible Flowers Vinegar
$^1/_3$ cup honey
1   cup vegetable oil
$^1/_2$ teaspoon paprika
$^1/_2$ teaspoon powdered mustard
$^1/_2$ teaspoon salt
$1^1/_2$ teaspoons minced lemon-scented
    herb (lemon verbena,
    lemon balm, lemon basil
    or lemon thyme)

Combine all ingredients in bowl;
mix well. Chill, covered, for
1 hour. Pour dressing over favorite
fruit salad and toss to coat.
You may substitute grated zest
of 1 lemon for the minced herb.

Yields 2 cups

Pepper Garlic Herb Vinegar Savory Dressing

$^1/_3$ cup Fredericksburg Pepper
    Garlic Herb Vinegar
1   teaspoon prepared Dijon mustard
1   teaspoon Tabasco sauce
$^1/_2$ tablespoon fresh lemon juice
1   tablespoon chopped parsley
$^1/_4$ teaspoon salt
$^1/_4$ teaspoon freshly ground
    mixed peppercorns
1   cup extra-virgin olive oil

Combine vinegar, Dijon mustard,
Tabasco sauce, lemon juice, parsley, salt and peppercorns in food
processor or blender container.
Process until well mixed. Add
olive oil gradually, mixing well.
Bottle and store in refrigerator.

Yields 1 bottle

Basil Blush Sweet Fruit Vinaigrette

$^1/_3$ cup Fredericksburg Basil
    Blush Herb Vinegar
$^3/_4$ cup sugar
$1^1/_2$ tablespoons Fredericksburg
    Fleurs de Provence Seasoning
1   teaspoon salt
1   teaspoon dried mustard
1   green onion, chopped
1   cup canola oil

Combine vinegar, sugar, seasoning,
salt, mustard and green onion in
food processor or blender container. Process until well mixed.
Add oil gradually, mixing well.
Bottle and store in refrigerator.

Yields 1 bottle

Herb and Flower Mayonnaise

3   tablespoons parsley leaves
1/3 green onion, chopped
1   clove of garlic, minced
1   egg
1   teaspoon Fredericksburg
     Edible Flowers Vinegar
1/8 teaspoon Tabasco sauce, or to taste
1/4 teaspoon salt
1/4 teaspoon ground white pepper
1   teaspoon Fredericksburg Fleurs
     de Provence Seasoning Mix
2   tablespoons edible flowers
     (if available, chive blossoms,
     nasturtiums, pansies and
     rose petals)
3/4 cup canola oil

Combine parsley, green onion, garlic, egg, vinegar, Tabasco sauce, salt, pepper, seasoning and flowers in food processor or blender container. Process until well mixed. Add oil gradually, mixing well. Bottle and store in refrigerator. Add up to 2 tablespoons additional Edible Flowers Vinegar for lighter consistency and more herb flavor.

Yields 1 bottle

Herbs de Provence Vinaigrette

1/4 cup Fredericksburg Herbs de
     Provence Seasoning Mix
2/3 cup Fredericksburg Basil,
     Scarborough Fair or Lovely
     Lemon Herb Vinegar
1   tablespoon dry white wine
2   cups cooking oil (your favorite)

Combine all ingredients in bowl; mix well. Let stand overnight. Bottle and store in refrigerator.

Yields 1 bottle

Sweet Balsamic Dressing

2   green onions, finely chopped
1/3 cup Fredericksburg
     Balsamic Vinegar
1/3 cup sugar
1   teaspoon dry mustard
1   teaspoon salt
3   cloves of garlic, minced
3   tablespoons chopped fresh basil
1   tablespoon chopped fresh oregano
1   cup canola oil

Combine green onions, vinegar, sugar, dry mustard, salt, garlic, basil and oregano in food processor or blender container. Process until well mixed. Add oil gradually, mixing well. Bottle and store in refrigerator.

Yields 1 bottle

Italian-Style Herb Vinaigrette

1/3 cup Fredericksburg Herb Vinegar
1/2 tablespoon white wine
1/2 tablespoon Fredericksburg Herbs
       de Provence Seasoning Mix
1/4 teaspoon salt
1   cup canola oil
1/4 cup freshly grated
       Parmesan cheese

Combine vinegar, wine, seasoning and salt in food processor or blender container. Process until well mixed. Add oil gradually, mixing well. Fold in cheese. Bottle and store in refrigerator.

Yields 1 bottle

If you want to
be happy for a week,
take a wife. . .

If you want to
be happy all your life,
make a garden.

—Chinese Proverb

Creamy Basil and Chive Salad Dressing

Everyone always raves about this delicious dressing.

1   cup sweet basil leaves
1/2 cup snipped chives
2   cloves of garlic
3 1/2 tablespoons Fredericksburg
       Pepper Garlic Vinegar
1 1/2 teaspoons Worcestershire sauce
3/4 teaspoon dry mustard
1/2 teaspoon black mustard
1   cup mayonnaise
3/4 cup sour cream

Combine all ingredients in blender container. Process until smooth. Bottle and store in refrigerator.

Yields 1 bottle

Mozzarella and Tomato Salad

6   medium tomatoes, sliced
8   ounces part skim
        mozzarella cheese, sliced
1   large purple onion, sliced,
        separated into rings
$1/3$ cup Fredericksburg Olive Oil
3   tablespoons Fredericksburg
        Herb Vinegar
2   tablespoons chopped parsley
1   tablespoon chopped basil
        or $1/2$ teaspoon dried
1   clove of garlic, minced
$1/4$ teaspoon Fredericksburg
        Sans Sal Seasoning
$1/8$ teaspoon Fredericksburg
        Herb & Pepper Seasoning
$1/4$ teaspoon sugar
$1/4$ teaspoon salt

Arrange tomatoes, cheese and
onion on serving platter.

Combine olive oil, vinegar, parsley,
basil, garlic, seasonings, sugar
and salt in large bowl; whisk to
combine. Spoon over vegetables.
Chill, covered, for several hours.
Garnish with parsley.

Yields 2 to 4 servings

Spicy Peach Chutney

3   tablespoons crushed red chiles
        with seeds
2   pounds peaches, peeled, chopped
2   cups Fredericksburg
        Pepper Garlic Herb Vinegar
$1^{1}/4$ cups packed light brown sugar
$1/4$ cup lemon juice
1   medium white onion, minced
$1/2$ cup raisins
2   teaspoons mustard seeds
1   teaspoon ground ginger
1   teaspoon ground cinnamon
$1/4$ teaspoon ground allspice

Combine all ingredients in
saucepan. Bring to a boil; reduce
heat. Simmer for 45 to 60 minutes
or until sauce is thick, stirring
occasionally and skimming off
any foam that forms. Pour chutney
into sterilized jars, leaving
1/4-inch headspace. Process jars
in boiling water bath for 15
minutes. Remove and cool. If not
processed, chutney will keep in
the refrigerator for up to 10 days.

Yields 4 cups

Admire Your Garden

Once you've got your
garden planted and situated, plan
to spend many more hours
admiring, touching, smelling, even
nibbling your handiwork.

Don't let a lack of space,
or time, or green thumbs
stand in the way of creating
an herb garden.

There's a lovely one within you
just waiting to be born!

The Art of Preserving Herbs

The best time to harvest herbs for their leaves is just before they bloom, when they have increased amounts of volatile oils and are at their most flavorful and fragrant. Cut them on a dry day when the morning dew has dried but before the sun is too hot. Herbs to be used in cooking should be swished in warm, not hot, water and dried gently on towels.

Many herb gardeners like to snip off the blooms to keep the plants from becoming leggy and to promote new growth.

You should allow some of your herbs to bloom, however, to attract butterflies and in order to use the blossoms in recipes and as garnishes.

You may enjoy hanging bunches of herbs to dry in your kitchen for decoration and aroma. They will serve that function well, but should not be used for cooking, as they collect dust and lose color and flavor rapidly.

Always store herbs in the leaf form in an airtight container away from heat and light. Crush or grind them just before using to prevent loss of flavor.

Brown Bag-Drying: Tie several stems together, place them in a paper bag, and tie the bag around the stems. Punch a few holes in the bag for air circulation. Hang bag upside down in a dry place for ten days to two weeks. Strip the leaves from the stems and store them in airtight containers.

Screen-Drying: Arrange the leaves of thicker herbs such as basil and sage on screens. Place them in an unused dark room with good air circulation. Let dry for three or four days. Cover the herbs loosely with paper towels and let dry until no moisture remains. This is an especially good way to dry lemon verbena.

Oven-Drying: Arrange the herbs in a single layer on a baking sheet. Place them in a warm oven with the door ajar. Dry for ten to thirty minutes, depending on the size and thickness of leaves; overheating will destroy the oils which give the flavor and aroma to the herbs.

Microwaving: If care is taken, some herbs can be microwaved without loss of flavor and color. Arrange the herbs on a paper plate and cover with a paper towel or arrange between paper towels. Microwave on High for about one and one-half to two minutes, testing them for moisture after about one minute.

Freezing: Herbs can be frozen in whole leaves, sprigs, or minced. Arrange whole leaves or sprigs on baking sheets and freeze for several hours. Package them in small quantities to use in cooking. The thawed herbs must be used immediately and cannot be used for garnish.

You can also place chopped herbs in the sections of an ice cube tray and fill with water to freeze. Remove frozen cubes and store in sealable plastic bags until needed for soups and stews.

Sorrel is best preserved if it is sautéed in butter with the water that clings to it after washing. Cool and freeze the mixture to use in soups or as a side dish. Flowers and freshly chopped herbs frozen in ice cubes or white grape juice will also add sparkle to punches and iced teas.

Salting: Layer the herbs with salt in a pan. Let stand until dry. Store both the herbs and the herb-flavored salt to use in cooking.

In Oil: Place the dried leaves of herbs such as basil in a jar of olive oil, safflower oil, sunflower oil, or walnut oil. Let stand in a warm place for several weeks before using. You can then use both the herb and the herb-flavored oil in cooking. Good choices for flavoring oils are rosemary, basil, tarragon, thyme, roasted garlic, cilantro, and marjoram.

Garlic must be roasted, and herbs must be completely dried to prevent the possibility of botulism.

Edible Flowers

Edible flowers are far from being a new concept; traditions of flower cookery come to us from the Victorian era and go back as far as the Roman Empire. We have been cooking and experimenting with edible flowers for four years and have gotten really excited about their potential as seasonings and garnishes. We use them under butter pats, on top of cakes, and in salads, soups, ice cream, and breads. Like all herbs and vegetables, flower blossoms must be well washed and pesticide free. Chemical fertilizers are safe but alter the flavor. We strongly

recommend using only organic fertilizers. Make sure you don't pick the wrong flowers!

Here are some tips for using edible flowers:

❧ Use lavender or roses to flavor jams and jellies.

❧ Decorate the top of an iced cake with mild-flavored fresh flowers like pansies, roses, dianthus or Johnny-jump-ups, or calendulas.

❧ Decorate and freshen up your plain tossed green salad with rosemary blossoms, chive blossoms, borage blossoms, nasturtiums, Johnny-jump-ups, or calendulas.

❧ Freeze borage blossoms or Johnny-jump-up blossoms into ice cubes for a beautiful accent to party punches or just plain ice water!

The Art of Preserving Flowers

Most flowers which are to be used in recipes or as garnishes are used fresh, but you may also want to dress up winter dishes with dried flower buds.

There are several methods for drying flowers for arrangements and potpourri, but flowers which are to be eaten should be grown and dried without chemicals.

Harvest the flowers when they are at their prime and choose the method that seems to work best for you.

Wash and gently dry edible flowers.

Air-Drying: This is probably the easiest and most often used method of drying flowers, especially if they are to be eaten. Strip the leaves from the flower stems and tie the stems together in bundles of about ten stems, unless the flower heads are very large. Hang the bundles upside down in a dry, dark place. Let hang until dry. This is also a good way to dry the flowering heads of herbs.

Microwaving: Cut the stems of flowers to be dried one-half inch long. Spread a one-half-inch deep layer of clay-based cat litter in a glass dish. Place three or four flower heads at a time face up in the litter. Place the glass dish in the microwave oven; place one cup of water in the corner of the microwave. Microwave flowers on High for one to three minutes, depending on the size and moisture content of the blooms. Let stand for one hour to overnight. This method works well with most blooms that are not too fleshy.

In Silica Gel: This is a drying agent found in garden centers under the name Flower-Dri. For this method, place the flower heads face up in a glass container. Sprinkle a layer of the gel over the flowers, covering completely. Let dry for four to seven days, checking occasionally to prevent flowers from becoming brittle. Dry the gel in the oven to reuse. Most flowers can be dried by this method for potpourri. Edible flowers that can be dried in this manner are calendula, lavender, marigold, pansy, rose, and sage.

Natural Drying: This easy method simply consists of collecting the flower heads or pods as they dry naturally at the end of the season. It is not the ideal method for flowers that need to retain their color, but it is ideal for ornamental grasses, sea oats, milkweed and poppy pods, and mosses and dock.

Pressing: Pressing flowers is a good way to retain their colors. Place a layer of newspapers on the floor of a warm dry area. Arrange the flowers with sides not touching in a single layer on the newspapers.

Aromatic Flower Arrangements

Allow some of the herbs in your garden to flower and bring the fragrance inside for a summery flowering herb arrangement.

Cut the herbs in midmorning after the dew dries and before the sun becomes too warm.

Place them in warm water for several hours to condition them.

Arrange them in an oasis to use on the table or in any room in the house or place them on a patio to attract butterflies.

Bruise a few of the lower leaves to release their special fragrance.

Some of the flowering herbs you can use are oregano, rose geraniums and lemon geraniums, mint, fennel, dill, basil, garlic, and summer savory.

Top with a sheet of plywood; weight with bricks. Let stand until dry. You may dry several layers of flowers at one time, placing plywood between each layer. This method is also used with ferns, grasses, and leaves.

Oven-Drying: To prepare flowers for tea, pull the petals from the flower heads and spread them on a screen. Let stand away from direct sunlight until dry, turning occasionally. If petals have not dried after several days, place in a 200-degree oven with the door ajar for several minutes until they are completely free of moisture. Cool completely and store in airtight containers in a cool dry place. Flowers with strong distinctive fragrances such as marigold, rose, yarrow, jasmine, and chamomile are good for teas. The flavor and fragrance will be released by steeping one teaspoon of the dried petals in a cup of boiled water for five to ten minutes.

Vinegar for the Bath

Adding a cup of cosmetic/tonic vinegar to your bath water will help to soothe, relax, and clean your skin—your skin will love you!

2 ounces rosemary
2 ounces rose petals
2 ounces lavender
2 ounces mint
2 ounces rose geranium
6 cups apple cider vinegar
   or white vinegar
1 cup rose water

Mix herbs and flowers together; add vinegar. Bottle and steep in refrigerator for 3 to 6 weeks. Strain and rebottle. Add a few fresh herb sprigs and the rose water.

Friends

A Positive Attitude: When we feel better about ourselves emotionally, physically, and spiritually, we do look younger.

Get into the fresh air as much as possible.

Exercise to improve circulation, actually encouraging thinning skin to thicken!

Eat fresh vegetables, fruit in moderation, grains, carbohydrates, and fish. Drink herbal teas and plenty of mineral water.

Always touch your face gently. Tomato slices help remove black-heads—drape over your nose, chin, and forehead for ten minutes.

Vodka makes a good pore-tightening toner for oily skin. Mother Nature's juice—water—is the best hydrator. Splash your face ten times after washing. Apply moisturizer immediately to damp skin.

Enemies

Our Emotions: Under stress? Not enough rest? Your skin may become dry and taut. Remember: You will look as worn out as you feel—physically, emotionally, and spiritually.

Hormonal Changes: Spots and blemishes, as well as increased oiliness with dry patches, may result.

Climate: Hot weather and or central heating can produce lumps and bumps as well as dryness and wrinkles. Similarly, cold weather can cause moisture to evaporate from your skin.

Cigarette Smoke and Air Pollution: Nothing ages a face faster—making it gray and wrinkled.

Pollution in the Diet: Alcohol, coffee, tea, sweets, and red meats.

Sun Abuse: Only potatoes were meant to be baked.

Personal Care: Avoid detergent-based cleansers; hot tap water and hard scrubbing to cleanse; rough textured washcloths; and direct heat on the face—including that from blow dryers.

Essential Oils

Where does smell, heavenly or otherwise, come from?

In flowers, it's captured in essential oils in the cells on the top of their petals, and released into the air in minute quantities—the warmer the air, the speedier their discharge. (To sniff a flower on a cool, breezy day, hold it close to your nose and gently breathe into it. The warmth of your breath will release the fragrant oil.)

The scent of most herbs is contained in their leaves, where tiny cells of essential oils can often be seen as pin-prick-like dots when the leaf is held against the light. Some scents are released by bruising or brushing the leaf as the oil-containing cells are buried deep. In thyme leaves, the scent is released simply by the heat of the sun. In fact, the oils and the tough surfaces of the leaves of rosemary, thyme, savory, and other Mediterranean herbs act like a suntan oil, protecting against the hot summer sun. Some plants, however, are fragrant only when dried—such as sweet woodruff's unmistakable new-mown hay aroma.

When both the flowers and the leaves of a plant are scented, the leaves are the more heavily perfumed. Not only that, but their fragrance lasts longer and intensifies with age, usually increasing when dried—moisture continues to evaporate from the leaf cells, concentrating the essential oils left behind. The opposite is true for flowers. As they age, they become less fragrant (some even become offensive, such as those which contain indole, a substance present in the early stages of putrefaction).

Steam Facial for Oily Skin/Large Pores

Springtime isn't just for cleaning house! Give yourself a lift with an herbal steam facial.

1   tablespoon comfrey leaf,
        cut, sifted (a healing herb)
2   tablespoons lavender flowers
        (a stimulant to normalize
        pore activity)
3   tablespoons powdered licorice root
        (a stimulant to normalize
        pore activity)
1   tablespoon lemon peel,
        cut, sifted (an astringent)
1   tablespoon peppermint, cut
        or whole (a restorative)
1   tablespoon pansy, cut
        or whole (a healing herb)

1   tablespoon parsley (a restorative)
1   tablespoon rose bud or
        leaf (an astringent)
1   tablespoon strawberry
        leaves (a restorative)
2   to 3 cups water

Combine all herbs in bowl; mix well. Place 1/4 cup mixture in tall narrow enamel or glass pot. Add water; cover pot. Bring to a boil. Simmer for 3 to 5 minutes; remove from heat. Steep for several minutes.

Cover hair with towel and remove lid from pot. Position face over pot (not too close). Cover pot and sides of face with the towel. Allow the herbal steam to relax, cleanse, and medicate your pores. Wipe away dirt and oil with clean washcloth, splash warm water on your face, and rinse with cool mineral water to close pores. Pat dry.

Potpourri

Potpourri is an appropriate gift for all occasions. Consider a container or sachet of aromatic potpourri for a holiday remembrance, a welcome hostess gift or house-warming gift, or a meaningful shower gift for bride or baby. With so much blooming in the garden, who can resist creating a personal blend with a pleasing natural scent to be enjoyed by all who visit your home! The spring garden potpourri is a light floral blend of pleasantly muted colors; the herb garden potpourri is for stress relief. Be sure that any materials harvested from the garden are completely dried to a crisp-papery consistency before using.

Herb Garden Potpourri for Stress Relief

1	ounce powdered orris root
6	drops of rosemary oil
6	drops of lemon oil
6	drops of lavender oil
6	drops of orange oil
2¹/₂	cups lemon verbena
1¹/₂	cups lemon balm
1	cup rosemary
1	cup lavender
¹/₂	cup thyme
¹/₂	cup sage
	Rose petals
	Yarrow blossoms
	Bay leaves
¹/₄	cup cinnamon powder
¹/₄	cup lovage root
6	tablespoons grated orange peel

Mix orris root and oils in small bowl; set aside. Combine lemon verbena, lemon balm, rosemary, lavender, thyme and sage in large bowl. Add a handful of rose petals and yarrow blossoms. Sprinkle in the bay leaves. Add cinnamon, lovage and orange peel. Stir in orris root mixture; cover bowl. Let stand out of direct light for 5 days, stirring occasionally. Place potpourri in smaller bowls or baskets and place near your bed or sofa.

Spring Garden Potpourri

2	ounces pink roses
1	ounce whole spearmint
2	ounces red roses
1	ounce feverfew flowers
1	ounce lavender
³/₄	ounce blue malva flowers
1	ounce oakmoss
1	large tonka bean, finely cut (acts as the fixative)
³/₄	ounce lemon verbena leaves, cut
3	drops each of rose oil, gardenia oil, and lavender oil

Combine all ingredients in bowl; mix well. Allow to age for several days. Use as desired.

The Creation of Calm

In the beginning, humans were led by their noses. To relieve muscle aches, to repel insects, and to hide their human scent from animals they feared or hunted, people rubbed strong-smelling herbs on their bodies. The sweet-smelling herbs attracted their mates and pleased themselves. Consider this regimen in an ancient Greek poem:

> His jaws and breasts he rubbed
> with thick palm oil,
> Both arms and buttocks
> with oily extracts of sweet mint.
> His brows and hair he powders
> with marjoram,
> His knees and neck he soothes
> with oil of thyme.

Sure to result in a beautiful body—or a fine pot roast! The ancient Egyptians generously basted their bodies and homes with aromatic oils. Priests embalmed their Pharaohs and, in their role as "psychiatrists," treated manias, depression, and nervousness with aromatic oils. Impressed, the Greeks and Romans used the Egyptians' knowledge to burn flowers, grasses, fruits, leaves, roots, and trees as scented sacrificial offerings to their gods—hence, the word perfume, from the Latin meaning "through smoke." Hippocrates, the father of medicine, prescribed "the way to health is to have an aromatic bath and scented massage every day." Delight and interest in plant fragrances literally wafted across the Mediterranean world.

Although the enthusiasm for cosmetic plant essences weakened in Europe during the Middle Ages, by the time of the fourth Crusade in 1202, France had taken alcohol-based perfume-making to heart and was the established center in Europe. Fragrant, but expensive, charms of aromatic oils reportedly rescued those of the upper class who made and used them to survive the ravages of many plagues. Yet even the peasants knew how to scent their homes by throwing a few sprigs of herbs on the hearth fire or by strewing fragrant branches on the floor. Herbs were the Procter and Gamble of the medicine chest, home, and personal care.

Good Herbal Body Scents

❧ For bathing—Angelica, mint, rosemary, and thyme. Add the herbs directly to the water, or place them in a small cheesecloth. Use very hot water, and let the herbs steep for ten minutes. Hop in and enjoy.

❧ As breath fresheners— Chew on a sprig of mint or parsley.

❧ In potpourri and sachets— Mints, thyme, rosemary, sage, dill, and savory. Combine the freshly dried herbs from your garden and let them sit in a closed container for the scents to mature and blend. To make sachets, grind the herbs into a powder and place in a small fabric bag. Use the sachets in drawers to give clothing a natural fragrance. To use as potpourri, place the herb mix in an open, pretty container to scent the room.

Gardener's Relaxing Footbath

After working in your herb garden, try this great pampering for your poor aching feet!

1	quart water
1/4	ounce bay leaves
1/4	ounce lavender flowers
1/4	ounce rosemary
1/4	ounce sage
1/4	ounce thyme
1/4	ounce lovage

Warm water in ceramic or porcelain pan. Add herbs when water boils; remove from heat. Let stand, covered, for 20 to 30 minutes. Filter the herbs; pour infusion into large bowl. Immerse feet for at least 15 minutes. Add a little more hot water if infusion begins to cool. Dry your feet completely. Massage with Fredericksburg Peppermint Foot Lotion.

Herbal Mouthwash

Use after meals to rinse and freshen your breath—it's sure to land you a kiss from that special someone!

3	cups spring water
1	ounce fresh lemon verbena
1	ounce fresh peppermint
1	ounce fresh rosemary

Bring water to a boil in saucepan. Add herbs; remove from heat. Infuse until cool. Filter off herbs; bottle and label.

Headache Pillow

2   parts lavender
1   part each lemon, thyme,
        lemon verbena and woodruff

Add a pinch of rosemary to each
pillow.

Sinus Pillow

2   parts crushed pine needles
1   part each rosemary and
        lemon verbena

Use a closely woven material for
pine needles—sharp pieces
emerging through the cover don't
make for restful sleep!

No Problem Skin

Cleanse gently twice a day with
a cleansing cream or lotion.
Follow every cleansing with a
mild freshener to keep your pores
tight and to remove all traces
of the cleanser.

⁓ Use a night cream on
rough, dry patches—when they
occur. Guard against the drying
aging effects of the sun by using
a sunscreen.

⁓ Once every two weeks,
stimulate the circulation and
smooth the surface of the skin by
using a mask.

⁓ It's no good taking care
of the face as if it were a rose
if the stalk cannot support it; the
bit you don't see in the mirror
as often—your body—will show
its age too quickly if not treated
with care, too.

Wrinkles

Our faces are like books—they tell a story. Each wrinkle represents a chapter in our lives,
and each blemish tells a story of misuse. Laughter lines tell the world that our lives contain humor.

The Secret Garden

No matter our age, we look for paradise, for a spiritual haven. Secret gardens are enclosed private places. There is usually a gate or door and one certain imperative: finding the key. When full of flowers and herbs symbolic of faith, hope, and love, and with gentle scents attractive to wildlife as if in the Garden of Eden, the cares and chaos of modern lifestyles are healed. Unlike haphazard nature, an enclosed garden is ours to design, ours to express personal needs. So drop your limitations at the gate and suspend time—a secret garden gives us a chance to create the moment, to labor or to relax, to believe in the impossible.

Our visit ends with the Secret Garden chapter, which emphasizes the romantic and sentimental side of life. We've included lots of ways to grow and use roses and have tucked in some terrific "feel-good" tips. We conclude with a number of recipes for sensuous desserts.

The Garden of Sentiment

Victorian gardens spoke! Fragrant small bouquets (tussie-mussies)

"There's no use trying," she said; "one can't believe impossible things."

"I daresay you haven't had much practice," said the Queen.

"When I was your age, I always did it for half-an-hour a day.

"Why, sometimes I've believed as many as six impossible things before breakfast."

—Lewis Carroll,
Through the Looking Glass

were a favorite floral harvest; flowers held hidden messages, but none spoke with more magical charm or authority than the rose.

The message was love, and roses held many romantic meanings for genteel Victorians, who used the "language of flowers" printed in nineteenth century etiquette books. One had to be selective. The gift of a single red rose signified "I love you." A proper Victorian lady might reply with a single yellow rose, which implied that her admirer was fickle; a white rose bud, which told him, "I am too young to love"; or a single rose leaf, which meant "I care not." If the suitor was really a gentleman, he would sign off with a musk rose, which meant "Thou art a capricious beauty." But if his original red rose elicited another red rose in reply, a match was made!

In the twentieth century, Samuel A. Binson published *Phyllanthography*, which contained a code devised to express names and thoughts through the arrangement of the flowers. The letters of the alphabet were represented by special groupings of leaves, buds, and blossoms so that short messages, such as *I love you* or *meet me in the garden*, could be silently conveyed by those who knew the language of roses.

For those who would like to grow roses simply because "their silent beauty speak," consider cultivating a Garden of Sentiment. Select plants from our unofficial (and very abbreviated) list of old roses and their sentiments, and coordinate with your landscape needs.

Or adapt this square design. There are roomy corners for vigorous growers—and many of the old roses are! Center planting of Baronne Prevost, Paul Neyron, Reine des Violettes—hybrid

perpetuals—are suggested for their intense rose fragrance, continuous blooming beauty (heavy in spring, sporadic during summer, re-flowering in the fall), and relatively undemanding habits (maintained with moderate pruning). By arching the corners of the center beds, space was made for a center of interest—a sundial, bird bath, or favorite statue—to be surrounded by low-growing roses such as Cecile Brunner or Marie Pavié. This same arc is repeated in each long side bed. Symmetry is emphasized at each of these arcs with three rose plantings of moderate growth height—possibly

Banshee, Mutabilis, or Marquise Boccella. Each end of the garden is balanced by selecting similar rose landscape forms—high hedge, or pillar-like growth such as Sombreuil, Souvenir de la Malmaison climbing, and Zephirine Crouhin. For an edging, use granite rock or railroad ties for appealing, fuss-free garden definition. Brick paving the pathways adds an air of formality; crushed gravel makes a more natural complement to the roses. A fence, picket or log, to add visitor privacy and to support a number of climbing old rose bushes completes this sentimental garden.

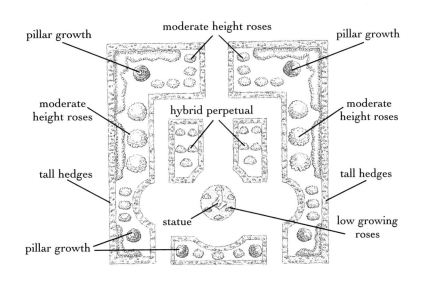

pillar growth · moderate height roses · pillar growth · moderate height roses · hybrid perpetual · moderate height roses · tall hedges · tall hedges · statue · low growing roses · pillar growth

Favorite Old Roses

Roses for Climbing Posts/Gazebos/Tall Hedges

Plant	Scent	Flower Color	Sentiment
Baronne Prevost, Hybrid Perpetual	Very perfumy	Big open flowers, many tight-packed soft rose-pink petals	Secrecy
Lady Banks'	Violets	Yellow, thornless	Joy, gladness
		White, thornless	Reverence, humility
Maggie	True rose, heady indoors	Rich carmine	Bashful shame
Mermaid	Sweet floral	Sulfur to buff yellow	Jealousy
Reve d' Or	Rich perfume	Buff yellow, nearly thornless	Sociability
R. Eglanteria/ Sweet Briar	Sweet apple-scented leaves	Clear pink	Sympathy
R. Moschata/ Musk Rose	Allspice, cloves, honey	Single creamy white blossoms	Capricious beauty
R. Multiflora, 'Platyphylia'/ Seven Sisters	Indistinct fragrance	Variety in each cluster, carmine to purple, mauve to pink and cream	Grace
Sombreuil	Delicious tea	Creamy white	Always lovely
Souvenir de la Malmaison, climbing	Fine rose scent	Pale flesh pink, large flat quarter blossoms	Queen of Beauty & Fragrance
York & Lancaster, Damask	Light rose scent	Bi-colored, white to pink-red double blossoms	War
Zephirine Drouhin	Raspberry-like	Vivid cerise-pink, thornless	Appreciation, attachment

Roses for Medium Height Design Areas

Plant	Scent	Flower Color	Sentiment
Archduke Charles, China	Indistinct	Crimson with neat pink center	Beauty always new
Autumn Damask '4 Seasons Rose of Paestrum'	Rich Damask perfume	Light pink, profusely double	Freshness
Banshee Damask	Penetrating Eau de Cologne	Pale pink, deepens in center, thornless	Friendship
Charles de Mills	Heavy, fruity fragrance	Rich crimson to purple tint	Unconscious beauty
Gloire des Mousseuse, Moss	Slight to moderate rose scent	Clear bright pink, deeper center, large cluster blooms	Superior merit
Kazanlik, Damask	Heady rose	Deep pink petals, halo of gold stamens	Brilliant complexion
La Reine, Hybrid Perpetual	Wonderful heavy rose	Silvery rose-pink, lilac overtones	Gratitude
Marquise Boccella, Hybrid Perpetual	Pure and sweet	Clustered, delicate pink packed-petals, folded inside	Sympathy
Mutabilis/ 'Butterfly Rose'	Indistinct	Sulfur yellow to orange, rich pink, crimson	Gaiety, joviality
Old Blush/ 'Old Pink Daily'	Soft and fruity	Lilac pink	Thy smile I aspire to
Paul Neyron/ 'Cabbage Rose,' Hybrid Perpetual	Slight to moderate scent	Rich pink	Ambassador of love
Reine des Violettes, thornless, Hybrid Perpetual	Outstanding rose scent	Soft violet	Early attachment
Swamp Rose	Very attractive	Soft to vivid pink	Admiration

Roses for Low Height Design Areas

Plant	Scent	Flower Color	Sentiment
Cecile Brunner	Light fragrant tea	Little pink buds	Young girl, 'The Sweetheart Rose'
Marie Pavié, thornless	Deliciously sweet	Sweetly-shaped pink bud to creamy white	The heart that knows not love
Souvenir de la Malmaison	Fine rose scent	Pale pink	Admiration

Growing Old Roses

First of all, just what is an "old rose"? Most collectors consider any rose "old" if it is seventy-five or more years old and it exhibits typical old rose characteristics—an unforgettable true rose perfume, a shrub form, muted blossom color, handsome foliage, and attractive hips in the fall. The final authority on this matter, at least within the United States, is the American Rose Society. The Society defines old roses as those that were grown before 1867, the year in which La France, the first of the Hybrid Tea Rose class, was released. Used synonymously with the term "old roses" are the terms "heritage roses" and "antique roses."

Sooner or later, most herb gardeners do try their hand at growing the old roses. Why? Briefly, because they have all the qualities that herb gardeners look for: fragrance, repeat colorful blooming (the more flowers, the merrier the garden), hardiness, and disease resistance. (Many varieties are resistant to diseases common to modern roses, such as black spot, mildew, and rust.) Equally important, however, is that the majority of old-fashioned roses do grow into low-maintenance bush shapes that have character. (And there is the added advantage of colored hips in the autumn.)

But somehow the idea that roses are difficult has crept into our horticultural-herb thinking, perhaps because we expect greater perfection from roses than from other plants. It's comforting to realize that the rose has been cultivated since the first gardener; it has existed as a wild plant in the Northern Hemisphere since the neolithic age! A monk in 1368 wrote that the "red rose is ye badge of England and hath growne in that countrye for as long as ye mynde of man goeth."

For the rose-herb garden, plants must have compatible cultural requirements. Know what you're planting; most roses are successful in a well-drained, deeply dug soil that has generous amounts of organic material. Roses need a minimum of six hours of direct sunlight and a spot where they will not compete with tree roots. Rose roots do go down deep into the soil, and they can withstand a certain degree of drought, although watering until they are established is critical. Ideally, soil should be prepared in the spring, allowing time for the soil to settle through the summer. Then the roses should be placed and planted in the late autumn.

Here is a partial list of herbs that grow well in the shade of roses; provide textural effect, contrast, or ground cover; or enhance a garden's romantic feel.

Alchemilla mollis (lady's mantle)

Allium Porrum group (leek)

Allium Aggregatum group (shallot)

Allium sativum (garlic)

Allium schoenoprasum (chives)

Artemisa abrotanum (southernwood)

Dianthus caryophyllus ('Essex Witch' dianthus)

Digitalis purpurea (foxglove)

Gysophilia paniculata (baby's breath)

Lavanula X intermedia ('Grosso lavender')

Ruta gravelolens ('Jackman's Blue' rue)

Salvia officinalis (purpurea sage)

Teucriuum chamaedrys (germander)

Viola odorata ('Royal Robe' violet)

Crystallized Roses

Rose petals
1   egg white, at room temperature
Few drops of water
1   cup superfine sugar

Rinse petals; pat dry. Beat egg white with water in a bowl until frothy. Using a small paint brush, coat each petal with egg white mixture. Sprinkle sugar evenly on both sides; mold petals back into original shape with toothpick. Place petals on waxed paper. Let stand for 12 to 36 hours or until dry. You may dry the petals in a 150- to 200-degree oven with the door ajar for several hours or place them in an oven with a pilot light overnight. Store in an airtight container for up to a year.

"There is always
room for beauty: memory

A myriad lovely
blossoms may enclose.

But, whatso'er hath been,
there still must be

Room for another rose."

—Florence Earle Coates,
The Poetry of Earth

Bottling Up the Rose

Nothing so awakens the pleasurable sensations of a flower as the subtle fragrance of rose water. Distilled from aromatic petals of "the Queen of Flowers," rose water holds a place of honor in true love's heart and draws us to previous generations as few other commodities can.

The scent of blossoming flowers has long challenged us to capture their delicate essence. Poetic legend tells us that rose oil was discovered by two lovers: Princess Nur Jahan and her Mogul emperor, Jehan Ghir, walked beside a canal in a garden and breathed in the sweet air. The canal had been filled with water and rose petals to honor their wedding day. On the surface of the water, they noticed thick, oily, butter-colored drops; these were skimmed off and found to be a heavenly attar. Exactly how the perfume was compounded was not recorded until the tenth century. Then Arab physician and

Luxurious Uses for Rose Water

For centuries, rose water has imparted its ethereal whisper to lotions, creams, and cuisines.

Rose water contains only purified water and the aromatic oil of the rose, so use it as often as you wish!

Rose water can be dabbed on the face to maintain a natural moisture balance, to soothe skin after shaving, and to remove the last traces of makeup and cleansing cream. It is beneficial for all complexion types.

Brush rose water through your hair to freshen it between shampoos.

Splash on lavishly after a bath or a long day; it's a natural hydrating agent for young-looking skin—the perfect body and soul rejuvenator.

philosopher Avicenna steeped summer's rose blooms in boiling water and succeeded in extracting their exquisite oil and creating the makings for rose water. With this happy result, the most fleeting fragrance could be contained for commerce.

Rose water has been esteemed since the time of Cleopatra, who is said to have safeguarded her legendary beauty by bathing in asses' milk scented with rose petals. Yet no one seems to have detailed such unabashed love of this water of the Queen of Flowers more than the herbals written during the reign of England's Elizabeth I. Its unmistakable delicate aroma, flavor, and cosmetic properties indulged the public's taste for sweetly scented foods, rooms, and clothes. Rose petals were also believed to have a purifying effect against diseases. John Gerard listed twenty-eight "virtues" of roses: among them, they will cure "the paine of the eies," give strength to the liver and kidneys, and bring "comfort to a weak stomake." Furthermore, "the distilled

Rose Symbolism

Red roses express love and respect

Deep pink ones,
gratitude and appreciation

Light pink, admiration and sympathy

The white rose, reverence and humility

The yellow, joy and gladness

The red and yellow blends, gaiety
and joviality

The light blended tones, sociability
and friendship

The orange tones, enthusiasm and desire

The China rose, grace or beauty ever fresh

The daily rose, a smile

The dog rose, pleasure mixed with pain

A faded rose, beauty is fleeting

The moss rose, voluptuous love

The musk rose, capricious beauty

The Provence rose, my heart is in flames

The white rose bud, too young to love

The white rose full of buds, secrecy

The yellow rose, infidelity

water of roses is good for strengthening the heart, & freshing the spirits." For "sweet water," the petals of cabbage roses and damask roses were exalted above all others. Elizabeth I also had a passion for rose water. She reportedly paid the large sum of forty pounds to a husband and wife named Kraunkewell, "stillers of sweet water." Rose water was cherished not only as a perfume; it was liberally sprinkled on floors and linen, freshening clothes which could not be easily laundered. Gerard observed, "The same [rose water] being put in dishes, cakes, sauces, and many other pleasant things giveth a fine and delectable taste." It often replaced doubtful well or stream water, and it was used in the wealthiest households for rinsing the hands.

Rose-Scented Sugar

Sugar
Rose petals

Fill clean pint jar 1/3 full with sugar. Sprinkle with a small handful of rose petals. Cover petals with enough of the sugar to fill the jar 2/3 full. Add another handful of petals and cover with the sugar, leaving 1/2-inch headspace. Seal with a lid; shake. Store in cool dark place for 2 to 3 weeks. The flavor of the sugar is enhanced with age. Replace the sugar as used; it will take on the fragrance of the rose petals.

"Scents are surer than sights or sounds to make the heartstrings crack."
—Rudyard Kipling

Topiary Treasures

Herb standards or topiaries are fragrant plants trained to grow with single stems into geometrically shaped forms. All topiary plants take time, but their rewards are great. For the patient gardener, a well-shaped topiary gives a wonderful sense of satisfaction and becomes a special personal treasure.

Topiaries were first introduced by the Romans; they reached the height of their popularity during the Renaissance period. At that time, almost every garden had a topiary; most gardens had more than one. They were grown in all shapes and sizes from simple to extravagant, from lollipops to pompoms, even in the shapes of amazing animals.

Growing topiaries gives you the opportunity to create your own miniature fairy tale garden — and in this age of hustle and bustle,

we can all benefit from a little make-believe! In fact, herbs are the subject of legend and folklore throughout the world. The silhouette of a simple topiary standard may often remind us of a child's drawing of a tree. Appropriately enough, a standard is a small tree symbolizing life, frequently planted at the birth of a baby.

Herbal topiaries can be any size, from six inches to several feet high, depending on the type of herb being trained and where the pot is to be kept. Interior decorators use small topiaries for their versatile decorative and fragrant values. They can lend formality and tradition, or they can add to a carefree and relaxing atmosphere. Placing a number of herbal topiaries inside your home on a window sill or a large table is a wonderful alternative to potpourri. Outside, they are ideal for landscaping the sides of a doorway, a balcony, a courtyard, or a patio.

Growing a topiary is an art and a craft; as with all creative projects, you must experiment and remember that practice makes perfect.

The following is a list of simple steps for growing your miniature fairy tale.

🌿 Choose your favorite herb. Good perennial herbs for topiaries are rosemary, myrtle, bay laurel, santolina, lavender, lemon verbena, curry, and some scented geraniums.

🌿 To start your topiary from a cutting, take a healthy straight twig or branch from the parent plant; dip the tip in rooting hormone; then plant the twig in a mixture of equal parts vermiculite, sand, and potting soil (Baccto is preferred). Water the cutting; place a plastic bag over the plant to create a miniature greenhouse until roots begin to develop. Put the cutting in an area where it will receive filtered sun for four to six hours per day — and remember to keep it moist! Roots and new leaves should start to appear in approximately three to four weeks. At this point, gradually give the plant more sun. If you start from a cutting, plan on at least a year before it begins to look like a topiary; plan on two to three years before it is completely finished.

Since topiaries must have good support from the very beginning, you will probably want to start your topiary from an established plant that has a single straight trunk. Firmly anchor to the bottom of your topiary's pot a 24-inch (or longer) bamboo or plastic-coated metal stake, alongside the plant's stem. Gently tie the stem and stake together with plastic-coated twist-ems, being careful not to tie too tightly; you want to avoid scarring the stem. Remove side branches at this time.

Initially, fertilize about every four to six weeks, depending upon the type of fertilizer used. Osmocote is excellent and lasts for a few months; a 20-20-20 water soluble fertilizer is good; but fish emulsion is considered best of all.

When the plant reaches the desired height, pinch out the head or growing tip so that two branches will form. Cut or pinch out the tips of the new branches that have formed from the growing tip. Multiple branching will develop if you continue pinching out the growing tips; eventually a desired round and bushy head will take shape.

Remember to develop the initial shape—give your topiary a regular haircut, especially during the early stages. Many people resist pruning, assuming that the growth of the plant is a sign of their good work, but all plants should be pruned or pinched back as they grow. It is part of routine care, like watering and fertilizing. Pruning energizes dormant growth buds while helping the whole plant to remain healthy.

Once the plant is a mature topiary, it will still need an occasional haircut to keep it neat and tidy. Pruning and clipping your herbs is a fragrantly delightful experience—as you clip, the sweet, natural smell of your herb's oil is released. Pruning can be relaxing, peaceful, and meditative if done in the right setting and with the right frame of mind.

Gertrude Jekyl, the twentieth century artist famous for her contribution to the art of perennial flower gardens, perhaps most accurately defined the art and craft of topiaries as "growing things as a means of expression in that domain of design that lies between architecture and gardening." Let topiaries be an inspiration for you to design your own personal fairy tale from nature's herbal greenery!

Quick Herb Bread

1¼ cups unbleached all-purpose
    flour
1½ cups whole wheat flour
½ cup yellow cornmeal
2 teaspoons baking powder
¾ teaspoon salt
½ teaspoon baking soda
2 tablespoons minced fresh basil,
    lemon verbena, tarragon or
    parsley or 2 teaspoons dried
1⅓ cups buttermilk
⅓ cup honey
¼ cup melted unsalted butter
1 egg

Mix flours, cornmeal, baking powder, salt, baking soda and herbs together in bowl. Combine buttermilk, honey, butter and egg in large bowl; mix well. Add flour mixture, stirring until just blended. Spoon into greased 5x9-inch glass loaf pan. Bake at 350 degrees for

1 hour or until loaf springs back when lightly touched. Cool in pan on wire rack for 10 minutes. Remove loaf to wire rack to cool to room temperature. Cut into slices. A mixture of 1/4 teaspoon each cinnamon, grated lemon peel and ground cloves may be substituted for the herbs listed; or you may substitute 1 1/2 teaspoons caraway seeds, poppy seeds or sesame seeds.

Yields 1 loaf

Secret Garden Menu

Quick herb bread

Mixed greens with dried herb dressing

Chicken soup with cilantro and cumin

Let them eat herb cake

Mixed Greens with Dried Herb Dressing

1 tablespoon (rounded)
    Fredericksburg Herbs de
    Provence or Pesto Seasoning
½ green onion
1 egg
1½ teaspoons Fredericksburg
    Pepper Garlic or Scarborough
    Fair Vinegar
½ teaspoon mustard
    Tabasco sauce to taste
¼ teaspoon salt
⅛ teaspoon ground black pepper
¾ cup canola oil
4 cups mixed greens
½ cup julienned red bell pepper
½ cup julienned carrot
½ cup seedless grape halves
¼ cup toasted almonds

Combine herbs, green onion, egg, vinegar, mustard, Tabasco sauce, salt and black pepper in food processor or blender container. Add oil slowly with machine running. Arrange greens, red pepper, carrot, grape halves and almonds on individual salad plates. Serve with herb dressing.

Yields 4 to 6 servings

Chicken Soup with Cilantro and Cumin

1¹/₂ pounds chicken pieces or
    shank meat
4   large cloves of garlic, minced
1   yellow onion, chopped
1   small bunch cilantro or
    parsley, chopped
1   tablespoon salt
1   tablespoon cumin
1¹/₂ teaspoons coarsely ground
    pepper
8   cups (about) water
1¹/₂ cups barley or small pasta or
    2 cups frozen corn
2   carrots, sliced
¹/₄ cup chopped cilantro or parsley
1   tablespoon tomato paste
    (optional)
    Shredded Monterey Jack or
    Cheddar cheese

Bring chicken, garlic, onion, cilantro, salt, cumin, pepper and water to a boil in large stockpot. Simmer, covered, for 1 1/2 to 2 hours. Remove chicken from broth; chop chicken. Strain liquid; discard vegetables. Return chicken to broth in stockpot. Add barley, carrots, 1/4 cup cilantro and tomato paste. Simmer for 30 minutes to 1 1/2 hours or until vegetables are tender. Ladle into bowls. Sprinkle with cheese.

Yields 6 to 8 servings

Let Them Eat Herb Cake

1   cup flour
¹/₂ teaspoon baking powder
¹/₈ teaspoon salt
1   small sprig of lemon verbena
1   teaspoon lemon extract
¹/₂ cup sugar
¹/₂ cup unsalted butter, softened
2   eggs

Mix flour, baking powder and salt together. Combine lemon verbena, flavoring and sugar in food processor or blender container. Process until finely ground. Add butter; blend until creamy. Add eggs 1 at a time, mixing well after each addition. Fold in flour mixture. Pour into greased and floured 7-inch round or 8-inch square cake pan. Bake at 350 degrees for 20 to 30 minutes or until cake tests done. Cool in pan. Spread slices with jam or a dollop of whipped cream. You may substitute 2 small rose geranium leaves for the lemon verbena and 1 teaspoon almond extract for the lemon.

Yields 8 to 10 servings

Rosy Cooler

This is an excellent drink for summer garden parties, especially since it is not strong enough to go to your head too quickly!

1   bottle rosé wine
    Strongly scented white and
        pink rose petals
1/4 cup vodka
    Raspberries to taste
1   bottle carbonated mineral
        water or 7-Up

Chill wine and rose petals in a glass bowl. Add vodka, raspberries and lots of ice cubes. Chill for 1 hour. Add mineral water at serving time.

Yields 6 to 8 servings

May Wine Cocktail

8   sprigs of tender young sweet
        woodruff
1   bottle medium-dry German
        white wine (riesling, moselle
        or Rhine)
8   teaspoons raspberry syrup or
        framboise liqueur
    Johnny-jump-up flowers
    Sliced fresh strawberries

Gently bruise woodruff leaves between fingers. Place in the bottle of wine; recork. Steep in refrigerator for 8 hours or longer. Strain through a sieve, discarding leaves. Place 2 teaspoons syrup in each of 4 stemmed wine glasses. Fill almost to the rim with white wine; stir gently. Float a small flower and a strawberry slice on surface of each drink.

Yields 4 servings

Creamy Rose Spread

8   ounces cream cheese, softened
2   tablespoons finely chopped rose
        flowers
3   to 4 tablespoons confectioners'
        sugar

Combine cream cheese, flowers and confectioners' sugar in bowl; mix well. Spoon into small crock. Chill until serving time. Serve with your favorite crackers or breads.

Yields 1 cup

Rose Flower Jelly

3 1/4 cups rose petals
2 cups water
1/2 cup sugar
1 cup white grape juice
1 package powdered fruit pectin
3 cups sugar
1/4 cup rose petals

Remove bitter white parts of all the rose petals. Rinse petals and pat dry. Bring 3 1/4 cups rose petals, water and 1/2 cup sugar to a boil in glass or stainless steel saucepan; reduce heat. Simmer for 5 minutes, stirring occasionally. Remove from heat. Let stand, covered, for several hours to overnight. Strain syrup, discarding flowers. Combine syrup, grape juice and pectin in glass or stainless steel saucepan; mix well. Bring to a boil. Boil for 1 minute, stirring occasionally. Add remaining 3 cups sugar; mix well. Bring to a full rolling boil that cannot be stirred down. Boil for 1 minute. Remove from heat. Place remaining 1/4 cup rose petals in 4 hot sterilized 1-cup jars. Ladle jelly into the jars, leaving a 1/2 inch headspace; seal with 2-piece lids. Drape jars with a towel. Cool to room temperature and store in a cool place.

Yields 4 cups

Rose-Glazed Brie

1 (15-ounce) round Brie cheese
  Rose flowers
1 envelope unflavored gelatin
1/4 cup cold water
2 cups white wine

Remove rind from top of cheese, leaving a 1/2-inch border. Rinse flowers; pat dry. Arrange on and around Brie wheel. Soften gelatin in cold water. Combine gelatin and wine in saucepan; mix well. Cook until the gelatin dissolves, stirring constantly. Brush flowers and cheese with gelatin mixture. Chill until set. Serve with assorted crackers. You may substitute any cheese or a variety of cheeses for the Brie.

Yields 15 servings

Flower Power Fruit Dressing

2 tablespoons Fredericksburg
  Edible Flower Preserves
  Juice of 1 orange
1/4 cup vanilla yogurt

Soften preserves in microwave on Medium for 20 seconds. Combine with orange juice and yogurt in bowl; mix well. Serve chilled over fruit salad.

Yields 1/2 cup

Chocolate Rose Leaves

Brush the undersides of fresh rose leaves with melted sweet or semisweet chocolate. Chill until firm. Peel the leaves carefully from the chocolate when ready to use. Use as desired for garnishes.

"Won't you come into my garden? I would like my roses to see you."
—Richard Sheridan, 1751–1816

Spring Compote

This is my version of a fresh orange and strawberry compote. The gingerroot gives it a pleasant sharpness, while the coriander seems to enhance the fresh flavor of the fruits.

4   navel oranges
1   pint fresh strawberries
1   to 2 tablespoons sugar (optional)
1/2   cup fruity white wine (optional)
1   tablespoon freshly grated
      gingerroot or to taste
3   tablespoons chopped fresh
      coriander or cilantro

Peel and slice oranges over a bowl to catch juice. Add orange slices and strawberries to the bowl with the juice. Add sugar if strawberries are tart. Add wine, ginger and coriander; mix gently. Let stand for 1 hour.

Yields 6 servings

Cilantro Bean Salad

1   cup cooked kidney beans
1   cup frozen green peas, thawed
3/4   cup chopped green onions
1   stalk celery, chopped
1   small green bell pepper, chopped
1   cup chopped tomatoes
1/4   cup chopped fresh cilantro leaves
1/4   cup chopped fresh basil
1   tablespoon vegetable oil
1 1/2   teaspoons ground cumin
1/2   teaspoon Tabasco sauce
1   tablespoon Fredericksburg
      Pepper Garlic Herb Vinegar
      Large romaine lettuce leaves
4   ounces goat cheese, crumbled

Combine beans, peas, green onions, celery, green pepper, tomatoes, cilantro and basil in large bowl; toss gently. Add oil, cumin, Tabasco sauce and vinegar; toss gently. Arrange lettuce on salad plates. Spoon salad onto lettuce leaves. Sprinkle with goat cheese.

Yields 2 to 4 servings

In the Pink Rose Petal Salad

2   Belgian endives
1   head Bibb lettuce, torn
1/4   cup pine nuts
      Petals of 4 mature pink roses
1/4   cup light olive oil
6   tablespoons raspberry vinegar

Arrange endive leaves on 4 chilled salad plates. Sprinkle with Bibb lettuce, pine nuts and rose petals. Whisk olive oil gradually into vinegar in small bowl. Drizzle over salad. Serve immediately.

Yields 4 servings

Marinated Vegetable Salad

1/3 cup Gewürztraminer wine
1/4 cup fresh lime juice
1/4 cup fresh lemon juice
1/4 cup corn oil
1/2 teaspoon freshly ground pepper
2 teaspoons fresh tarragon
1/2 teaspoon fresh rosemary
1 or 2 cloves of garlic, chopped
1 green bell pepper, chopped
1 red or yellow bell pepper, chopped
1 large red onion, peeled, chopped
2 zucchini, chopped
1 1/2 pounds mushrooms, sliced
32 cherry tomatoes
Salt to taste

Combine wine, juices, oil, spices and garlic in large nonmetallic bowl; mix well. Chill for 2 hours to overnight. Add peppers, onion, zucchini and mushrooms; mix well. Marinate for 1 to 2 hours, stirring occasionally. Add cherry tomatoes and salt. Serve chilled or at room temperature.

Yields 6 to 8 servings

Basil Tomato Pie

We love this recipe—it helps slow the avalanche of fresh tomatoes we experience each summer.

2 cups flour
1/2 teaspoon salt
2 teaspoons baking powder
1/2 cup unsalted butter
1/3 cup milk
3 pounds ripe tomatoes, sliced
2 tablespoons finely chopped fresh chives
1/4 cup finely chopped fresh basil
3/4 teaspoon salt
1/2 cup shredded extra-sharp Cheddar cheese
2/3 cup mayonnaise
1/2 cup shredded extra-sharp Cheddar cheese

Combine flour, salt and baking powder in food processor container. Process briefly. Add butter; process until crumbly. Add milk. Process until dough forms. Divide dough into halves. Roll on floured surface. Fit half the pastry into a 10-inch pie plate sprayed with nonstick cooking spray. Mix tomatoes, herbs, salt and 1/2 cup cheese in bowl. Spoon into prepared pie plate. Spread mayonnaise over tomato mixture. Sprinkle with remaining 1/2 cup cheese. Top with remaining pastry, sealing edge and cutting vents. Bake at 350 degrees for 45 to 60 minutes or until browned and bubbly.

Yields 6 servings

Individual Herb Pies

Chervil, chives and parsley dot the creamy custard in this specialty.

1³/4 cups flour
¹/8 teaspoon salt
10 tablespoons chilled unsalted butter, cut into ¹/2-inch pieces
3 tablespoons shortening
¹/2 cup ice water
1 tablespoon unsalted butter
2 medium shallots, minced
2¹/2 cups whipping cream
1¹/4 teaspoons salt
¹/2 teaspoon freshly ground white pepper
¹/4 teaspoon freshly grated nutmeg
4 eggs
2 egg yolks
2 tablespoons minced fresh parsley
2 tablespoons minced fresh chives
1 tablespoon minced fresh chervil or 1¹/2 teaspoons dried, crumbled
2 tablespoons prepared English mustard

Butter eight 4-inch fluted tart pans with removable bottoms. Sift flour and 1/8 teaspoon salt into bowl. Cut in 10 tablespoons butter and shortening until crumbly. Add ice water; stir just until dough forms. Shape into a ball. Chill, wrapped in plastic, for at least 1 hour; dough may be prepared 2 days in advance. Flatten dough; cut into 8 pieces. Roll on floured surface into circles 1/8 inch thick. Fit into tart pans; trim excess. Chill for 1 hour. Line shells with foil or parchment; fill with dried beans or pie weights. Bake at 350 degrees for 20 to 25 minutes or until pastry is set and edges begin to brown. Remove beans and foil. Cool in pans on wire racks. Melt remaining 1 tablespoon butter in heavy skillet over medium heat. Add shallots. Cook for 2 minutes, stirring constantly; do not brown. Add cream. Bring to a boil. Add remaining 1 1/4 teaspoons salt, pepper and nutmeg. Beat eggs and egg yolks in bowl. Whisk a small amount of hot cream mixture into eggs. Whisk eggs into cream mixture. Stir in parsley, chives and chervil. Brush pastry shells with mustard. Pour filling into shells. Bake at 350 degrees for 25 to 30 minutes or until custard is puffed and firm. Cool slightly.

Yields 8 servings

Tabouli

1 cup cracked wheat
1 cup (about) very warm water
1 bunch spring onions, finely chopped
3 cups finely chopped parsley
¹/2 cup olive oil
¹/3 cup lemon juice
1 large ripe tomato, peeled, chopped
2 cloves of garlic, minced
  Salt and pepper to taste
  Fresh lettuce leaves

Soak cracked wheat in water for 1 to 2 hours. Add next 8 ingredients; mix well. Chill for 8 hours or longer to allow flavors to blend. Spoon onto lettuce.

Yields 3 to 4 servings

Sémillon Herb Pie

2   pounds boneless chicken
      breasts, cut into strips
      Salt and pepper to taste
2   tablespoons fresh lemon
      thyme leaves
3/4   pound ground pork
3/4   pound ground turkey
4   slices bread, crusts trimmed,
      torn into pieces
1/4   cup Sémillon wine
2   tablespoons water
2   tablespoons chopped fresh
      lemon verbena leaves
      Grated zest of 1 lemon
2   eggs
1/2   teaspoon salt
1/4   teaspoon pepper
1   recipe (2-crust) pie pastry
1   egg yolk, beaten

Season chicken with salt and pepper to taste. Roll in thyme leaves. Mix pork, turkey, bread, wine, water, lemon verbena, lemon zest, eggs, 1/2 teaspoon salt and 1/4 teaspoon pepper in bowl. Roll 2/3 of the pastry 1/8 inch thick on floured surface. Line bottom and side of 9-inch springform pan with pastry. Layer turkey mixture and chicken strips 1/3 at a time in pan, ending with turkey mixture. Roll remaining pastry into a circle on floured surface. Fit over pie, sealing edge and cutting vents. Roll pastry scraps; cut into decorative pieces. Brush crust with egg yolk. Decorate with cutouts; brush with egg yolk. Bake at 325 degrees for 1 3/4 to 2 hours. Cover edge with foil if needed to keep pastry from browning too quickly. Cool on wire rack. Serve with Sémillon Wine Sauce.

Yields 6 to 8 servings

Sémillon Wine Sauce

2   tablespoons Sémillon wine
2   egg yolks
1   tablespoon grainy mustard
1   clove of garlic, minced
1   tablespoon chopped fresh dill
1   tablespoon chopped fresh parsley
1/4   teaspoon salt
1/8   teaspoon white pepper
1/2   cup extra-virgin olive oil
1/2   cup canola oil

Combine wine, egg yolks, mustard, garlic, dill, parsley, salt and pepper in food processor or blender container. Process until finely chopped and well blended. Add oils gradually with food processor running, allowing the sauce to thicken as oils are added. Add more wine if sauce is too thick.

Yields 1 1/2 to 2 cups

The rose is fairest
when 'tis budding new.

And hope is brightest
when it dawns from fears;

The rose is sweetest
washed with morning dew,

And love is loveliest
when embalmed in tears.

—Sir Walter Scott,
The Lady of the Lake

"The sense of smell is the sense of the imagination."
—Rousseau

Lemon Balm Bars

Pictured on page 163.

$1/2$ cup unsalted butter, cut into
         small pieces
$1/4$ cup confectioners' sugar
1 cup flour
$1/3$ cup blanched almonds
1 cup sugar
3 tablespoons flour
$1/2$ tablespoon lemon balm leaves
         Grated zest of 1 lemon
3 eggs
$1/3$ cup fresh lemon juice
2 tablespoons confectioners' sugar
$1/3$ cup blanched almonds

Combine butter, 1/4 cup confectioners' sugar, 1 cup flour and 1/3 cup almonds in food processor container. Process until mixture forms a ball. Pat into greased and floured 9x9-inch baking pan. Bake at 350 degrees for 20 minutes. Combine sugar, 3 tablespoons flour, lemon balm and lemon zest in food processor container. Process until finely minced. Add eggs and lemon juice; blend thoroughly. Pour over crust. Grind remaining 2 tablespoons confectioners' sugar and 1/3 cup almonds in food processor. Sprinkle over filling. Bake at 350 degrees for 40 to 45 minutes or until set.

Yields 9 large bars

Lemon Verbena Lace Cookies

$1/2$ cup sugar
3 tablespoons flour
$1/8$ teaspoon salt
$1^1/3$ cups sliced almonds
2 egg whites
2 tablespoons melted unsalted butter
1 tablespoon minced fresh
         lemon verbena
2 teaspoons grated lemon zest
$1/4$ teaspoon vanilla extract
$1/8$ teaspoon almond extract
$1/8$ teaspoon lemon extract
3 ounces semisweet chocolate,
         melted

Combine sugar, flour and salt in bowl. Add almonds; toss to coat. Stir in egg whites, butter, lemon verbena, lemon zest and flavorings; mix well. Chill, covered, overnight. Spread 1 tablespoon batter into a 3-inch circle on greased cookie sheet. Repeat with remaining batter, spacing cookies 3 inches apart; make only 4 cookies at a time. Bake at 350 degrees for 8 to 10 minutes or until edges are lightly browned. Loosen cookies from cookie sheet quickly. Curve over rolling pin or small inverted bowl immediately to shape and cool. Spread melted chocolate over cooled cookies.

Yields 4 cookies

Spicy Rain Forest Chip Cookies

These cookies earn their keep in lunch pails or backpacks. They travel well and sustain weary gardeners.

¹/₂ cup unsalted butter, softened
¹/₂ cup firmly packed light brown sugar
¹/₄ cup sugar
1 large egg
1 tablespoon warm water
¹/₂ teaspoon vanilla extract
1¹/₂ cups rolled oats
¹/₂ cup sweetened flaked coconut
¹/₂ cup roasted peanuts
¹/₂ cup golden raisins
1 cup semisweet chocolate chips
6 tablespoons unbleached flour
¹/₂ teaspoon salt
¹/₂ teaspoon baking soda
¹/₂ teaspoon cinnamon

Cream butter, brown sugar and sugar in mixer bowl until light and fluffy. Beat in egg, water and vanilla. Stir in oats, coconut, peanuts, raisins and chocolate chips. Add flour, salt, baking soda and cinnamon; mix well. Scoop and level off 1/3 cup of dough. Drop dough 4 inches apart onto greased cookie sheet. Bake at 375 degrees for 17 to 21 minutes or until golden brown.

Yields 2 dozen

Peppermint Shortbread

This is great with chocolate ice cream!

12 tablespoons unsalted butter, softened
9 tablespoons sugar
1¹/₂ tablespoons brown sugar
1 egg
¹/₄ teaspoon vanilla extract
³/₄ teaspoon peppermint extract
2 cups unbleached flour
1 tablespoon minced peppermint leaves
¹/₈ teaspoon salt or to taste

Cream butter, sugar and brown sugar in mixer bowl until light and fluffy. Beat in egg and flavorings. Add flour gradually, beating well after each addition. Stir in peppermint and salt. Mix until soft dough forms. Divide dough into 3 portions. Roll each portion into a 1 1/4-inch cylinder, using plastic wrap to shape the dough. Chill for 1 to 2 hours. Remove plastic wrap; cut dough into 1/4-inch rounds. Place on ungreased cookie sheet. Bake at 350 degrees for 8 to 10 minutes or until lightly browned. Remove hot cookies to wire racks to cool. Store in airtight container.

Yields 2 dozen

Varney's Fresh Peppermint Fudge Brownies

With these unconventional glazed brownies, Sylvia Varney surprises anyone who thinks that herbs and desserts don't mix.

1$^{1}/_{2}$ cups sifted flour
14   tablespoons baking cocoa
1   teaspoon salt
1   teaspoon baking powder
1$^{1}/_{3}$ cups margarine
2   cups sugar, sifted
4   eggs
2   teaspoons vanilla extract
2   tablespoons honey
2   cups coarsely chopped toasted
       pecans
2   cups confectioners' sugar
$^{1}/_{4}$ cup unsalted butter, softened
2   tablespoons milk
$^{1}/_{2}$ tablespoon finely minced fresh
       mint leaves or 1 tablespoon
       peppermint extract
3   drops of green food coloring
       (optional)
3   ounces unsweetened chocolate
3   tablespoons unsalted butter

Sift flour, cocoa, salt and baking powder together. Cream margarine and sugar in mixer bowl until light and fluffy. Add eggs 1 at a time, beating well after each addition. Stir in vanilla and honey. Add flour mixture gradually, beating well after each addition. Fold in pecans. Spread in greased and floured jelly roll pan. Bake at 350 degrees for 30 minutes or until center is solid. Mix confectioners' sugar, 1/4 cup butter, milk, mint and food coloring in bowl until of spreading consistency. Spread over cooled brownies. Place in freezer for 20 minutes. Melt chocolate with remaining 3 tablespoons butter in saucepan over low heat. Let stand to cool. Drizzle over frosting. Cut into squares.

Yields 2 dozen

Basil Pecan Sandies

1   tablespoon chopped cinnamon
       basil
$^{1}/_{4}$ cup sugar
1   cup butter
2   cups flour
       Salt and cinnamon to taste
1   cup chopped pecans
1$^{1}/_{2}$ teaspoons vanilla extract

Mince basil with sugar in food processor; set aside. Melt butter in large saucepan. Add sugar mixture, flour, salt and cinnamon. Stir in pecans and vanilla. Shape into 1/4-cup-sized balls. Place on ungreased cookie sheets. Press dough with bottom of large glass. Bake at 300 degrees for 40 minutes or until golden brown.

Yields 10 king-sized cookies

Chaucer's Love Dish

This condiment comes from the "Legend of the Good Woman" and is included in *To the King's Taste*, the cookbook prepared for Richard II by Lorna Sass in the fourteenth century.

¹/₄ cup dried crushed rose petals
1¹/₂ cups almond milk (blanched almonds soaked in milk)
¹/₂ teaspoon cinnamon
¹/₂ teaspoon ginger
2 teaspoons rice flour
2 tablespoons cold water
¹/₄ cup minced fresh dates
3 tablespoons pine nuts

Soak dried petals in almond milk for 10 minutes in saucepan. Add cinnamon and ginger. Cook over low heat for 5 minutes. Blend flour with water; stir into milk mixture. Add dates and pine nuts; mix well. Pour into 2 bowls. Garnish with fresh rose petals.

Yields 2 servings

Bleeding Heart Muffins

We used heart-shaped cast-iron muffin cups. If they are not available, you may use standard 2 1/2-inch muffin cups.

1³/₄ cups flour
2 tablespoons sugar
1 tablespoon baking powder
¹/₂ teaspoon baking soda
¹/₂ teaspoon salt
2 tablespoons packed brown sugar
1 tablespoon grated lemon zest
¹/₄ cup cold unsalted butter, cubed
1 egg
1 cup milk
6 tablespoons red fruit preserves
2 tablespoons minced fresh mint or lemon balm

Sift flour, sugar, baking powder, baking soda and salt together in bowl. Stir in brown sugar and lemon zest. Cut in butter until crumbly. Make well in center of mixture; set aside. Whisk egg with milk in small bowl until blended. Add to flour mixture, stirring just until moistened; do not overmix. Mix preserves with mint in small bowl. Spoon 1 tablespoon batter into each well-oiled muffin cup; if using standard size, fill 2/3 full. Spoon 1/2 teaspoon preserve mixture on each muffin. Swirl in zigzag pattern with wooden pick. Bake at 400 degrees for 15 to 16 minutes or until wooden pick inserted near center comes out clean; if using standard size, bake for 18 to 20 minutes.

Yields 30 heart-shaped muffins or 12 standard muffins

Rose Geranium Buttermilk Pies

1³/₄ cups unbleached flour
¹/₄   teaspoon salt
2   teaspoons sugar
10   tablespoons cold unsalted
       butter, cut into ¹/₄-inch pieces
3   tablespoons cold shortening, cut
       into ¹/₄-inch pieces
¹/₂   cup (or less) ice water
4   to 6 medium rose geranium
       leaves
2   cups sugar
¹/₂   cup unsalted butter, softened
6   eggs
2   cups buttermilk
¹/₈   teaspoon nutmeg or to taste

Combine flour, salt and 2 teaspoons sugar in food processor container. Add 10 tablespoons butter and

Myriad Uses of Roses

Don't restrict the use of roses in cooking merely to garnishes.

Make rose syrup or rose honey for fruit salads and breads.

Have rose sugar for sweetening cereals and baking.

Use rose butter for dainty sandwiches.

Make jelly with rose petals, jam with rose hips, for the prettiest treats.

Surprise guests with rose tea or rose punch.

For a touch of the eighteenth century in the twentieth, add pink petals to your pancake batter, puddings, or butter cookie dough.

Add petals to the top of cherries in a pie (an old, old secret?). A divine color will result with the reddest petals.

Freeze your nicest blooms in ice cubes for special drinks.

shortening. Process until crumbly. Add ice water with food processor running until mixture forms a ball. Turn out onto plastic wrap. Shape dough into large ball. Chill for 30 minutes or longer. Divide dough into 2 portions. Roll into circles on floured surface. Fit dough into two 9-inch pie plates; trim and flute edges. Mince leaves with 2 cups sugar in food processor. Add remaining 1/2 cup butter. Process until creamy. Beat in eggs, buttermilk and nutmeg. Pour into pie shells. Bake at 350 degrees for 50 minutes or until center is almost set. Cool completely.

Yields 6 to 8 servings

Rose Geranium Italian Cream Cake

It's been said that the cook who makes this cake will be as sweet as an angel, because all her sin goes into this dessert!

4   large rose geranium leaves
1/2 cup sugar
1   cup unsalted butter, softened
1   cup sugar
1/2 teaspoon salt
1 1/2 teaspoons vanilla extract
5   extra-large egg yolks, at room temperature
1   teaspoon baking soda
1   cup buttermilk
2   cups flour
5   extra-large egg whites, at room temperature
1/2 cup sugar
1   cup finely chopped pecans
1   cup sweetened flaked coconut
     Rose Cream Frosting

Mince geranium leaves with 1/2 cup sugar in food processor. Cream sugar mixture, butter, 1 cup sugar, salt and vanilla in mixer bowl until light and fluffy. Add egg yolks 1 at a time, beating well after each addition. Dissolve baking soda in buttermilk. Add buttermilk mixture and flour alternately to creamed mixture, beating well after each addition. Whip egg whites in small mixer bowl until soft peaks form. Add remaining 1/2 cup sugar gradually, beating constantly until stiff peaks form. Fold into batter. Stir in pecans and coconut. Pour into 3 greased and floured 9-inch cake pans. Bake at 325 degrees for 40 minutes or until layers test done. Cool in pans for several minutes. Remove to wire racks to cool completely. Spread Rose Cream Frosting between layers and over top and side of cake. Garnish with additional geranium leaves and rose buds or petals. This cake must be stored in the refrigerator if it is not eaten the same day it is prepared.

Yields 12 servings

Rose Cream Frosting

3/4 cup unsalted butter, at room temperature
12   ounces cream cheese, softened
1   teaspoon vanilla extract
1   drop of rose geranium essential oil
1 1/2 pounds confectioners' sugar

Cream butter, cream cheese, vanilla and essential oil in mixer bowl until light and fluffy. Add confectioners' sugar gradually, beating until of spreading consistency.

Yields enough frosting for a 3-layer cake

"How cunningly nature hides every wrinkle of her
inconceivable antiquity under roses and violets and morning dew!"
—Ralph Waldo Emerson

Rosemary and Orange Rum Cake with Glorious Glaze

Pictured on page 29.

1   (2-layer) package yellow cake mix
1   small package vanilla instant pudding mix
1   tablespoon finely minced fresh rosemary
     Grated zest of 1 orange
1/2 cup water
1/2 cup canola oil
1/2 cup light rum
4   extra-large eggs
1   cup chopped pecans
     Glorious Glaze

Combine cake mix, pudding mix, rosemary and orange zest in food processor or blender container. Process until mixed. Add water, oil and rum; mix well. Add eggs 1 at a time, mixing well after each addition. Stir in pecans. Pour into bundt pan sprayed with nonstick baking spray. Bake at 325 degrees for 1 hour or until wooden pick comes out clean. Pour Glorious Glaze over cake in pan. Allow glaze to soak into pan completely before removing cake. Invert cake so that glazed top is facing up. Garnish with long rosemary sprigs and pale blue pansies.

Yields 16 servings

Glorious Glaze

1/2 cup unsalted butter
1   cup sugar
1/4 cup water
1/4 cup rum

Bring butter, sugar, water and rum to a boil in saucepan. Boil until mixture reaches soft-ball stage or 235 degrees on candy thermometer.

Yields enough glaze for 1 cake

Mighty Mint Chocolate Cheesecake

1 1/2 cups vanilla wafer crumbs
3   tablespoons melted butter
1/4 cup baking cocoa
1   cup sugar
24   ounces cream cheese, softened
2/3 cup melted mint chocolate chips
2   ounces bittersweet chocolate, melted
3   tablespoons flour
3   eggs
2   egg yolks
1   cup heavy cream

Mix crumbs, butter and cocoa in bowl. Press into buttered 9-inch springform pan. Chill until baking time. Cream sugar and cream cheese in mixer bowl until light and fluffy. Stir in chocolate and flour. Add eggs and egg yolks 1 at a time, beating well after each addition. Blend in cream. Pour into prepared pan. Bake at 325 degrees for 1 hour and 5 minutes. Turn off oven. Let cheesecake stand in closed oven overnight. Chill for several hours.

Yields 12 servings

Tips for Using Fragrances

The chest, the torso, and the nape of the neck are better sites for applying fragrance than the pulse points.

🌿 Never store perfumes where they will be heated, and do not place them in sunlight.

🌿 Change your fragrance periodically; otherwise, in less than six weeks, you will be unable to smell it on yourself.

🌿 Your fingers can contaminate your fragrance, so use an atomizer or 100 percent pure cotton balls.

🌿 Be careful when applying perfume because the oil in it can cause spots on clothing. Because colognes have a large alcohol content, smelling a scent immediately after application will give you a noseful of alcohol!

🌿 Cologne and perfume of a certain fragrance will not smell the same—perfumes have a stronger reaction to body oils.

Love Potion

Particular combinations of flowers and herbs have traditionally been used to attract the opposite sex.

The mixture is placed in a small sachet and worn inside the clothing.

The combination used to attract a man includes equal parts of dried lavender, bachelor's buttons, and clary sage, with a pinch of valerian and a sassafras leaf.

To attract a woman, mix equal parts of dried rose petals, jasmine blossoms, patchouli, henbane, and cinnamon.

The Harem Body Scrub

One of the most luxurious and sensual body preparations comes from the East, where reputedly it was used to prepare women for the sultan's pleasure. It removes dead skin cells and leaves the skin glowing, fragrant, and soft.

1	teaspoon ground dried citrus fruit peel
1	tablespoon ground almonds
2	teaspoons oats
1	pinch of clove powder
1	teaspoon crushed dried rose petals
1	pinch of nutmeg powder
1/4	cup almond oil
2	drops of lemon or orange oil
2	drops of sandalwood oil

Blend all ingredients into a paste. Use your fingertips to massage into the skin in a circular motion and then rinse off.

Texas Hill Country HERB CHART

	Beef	Pork & Lamb	Fish & Poultry	Eggs & Cheese	Salads & Vegetables	Tex-Mex	German
Basil	Beef Stew	Broiled Lamb Chops	Fish or Chicken Italiano	Deviled Eggs Pesto (herbed sauce)	Stewed Tomatoes Zucchini Bread	Gazpacho	Kohlrou-laden (stuffed cabbage)
Chives	Beef Stroganoff	Fruited Pork Chops	Butter for Chicken / Seafood Bisque	Omelettes / Macaroni & Cheese	Baked Potatoes Fried Eggplant	Tacos Nachos	Speck-kloesse (bacon dumplings)
Dill	★	🐐	Baked Flounder Salmon Mousse	Yogurt Dip Cream Cheese Spread	Marinated Cucumber Cole slaw	Tamale Pie	Sauerkraut
Marjoram	Chili Con Carne	Lamb Kabobs	Lemon Chicken	Cheese Fondue	Green Bean Salad Minestrone Soup	Salsa / Mexican Rice	Sauer-braten (beef roast)
Mint	🐂	Baked Leg of Lamb	Honey Baked Chicken	Peppered Cheese Ball	Fruit Salad Fresh Pea Casserole	Margaritas Sangria	Appel-salat (apple salad)
Oregano	Spaghetti Lasagne	Roast Pork	Stewed Chicken	Cheddar Bread Pizza Topping	Broccoli & Rice Bake Ratatouille sauce	Chili Rellenos	Bohnen-suppe (bean soup)
Parsley	Burgers Stuffed Peppers	Irish Stew	Fillet of Sole Oyster Stuffing	Souffle Cheddar Soup	Caesar Salad Potatoes Lyonnaise	Guacamole	Wiener-Schnitzel (breaded veal cutlet)
Rosemary	Grilled Steaks	Barbecued Lamb	Chicken with white wine	Scrambled Eggs	Baked Squash Green Beans	Cabrito (roast goat)	Fried Potatoes
Sage	Marinade for Meat Salad	Sausage Stuffing	Baked Cornish Hens	Curried Eggs	Creamed Onions Tomato Soup	Chicken Enchiladas	Wurst (sausage)
Tarragon	Pot Roast	Grilled Lamb	Tomato & Fish Cocktails Chicken Salad	Quiche Cheese Stuffed Veges	Baked Artichokes Lettuce Salad	Seviche (fish salad)	❤
Thyme	Meat Loaf Beef Curry	Moussaka (ground lamb casserole)	Lemon Butter for fish	Egg Foo Young (Chinese omelette)	Mushroom Pate	Huevos Rancheros	Hasen-pfeffer (rabbit stew)

VARNEY'S · CHEMIST · LADEN

HERB SHED

Lee Ethel

© 1987 VARNEY'S CHEMIST LADEN, FREDERICKSBURG Tx.

Index

Photography

Front cover—A typical herbal
lunch at Fredericksburg
Herb Farm, looking into our
Secret Garden
©1995 Lynn A. Herrmann

Page 8—Lower left
Historic farmhouse
Photograph by Henry Lehne
family

Upper right—Path to retail shop
and tea room
Photograph by Texas Highways

Page 9—Entrance to
Fredericksburg Herb Farm
Photograph by Texas Highways

Page 10—Fredericksburg
Herbal Honeys
©1995 Lynn A. Herrmann

Page 12—A view of the Ichthus
Garden
Photograph by Texas Highways

Page 19—Tea and breads
©1989 David E. Kennedy

Page 29—Rosemary plants and
our Rosemary Orange
Rum Cake
©1995 Lynn A. Herrmann

Page 33—Guest room at the
Herb Haus Bed and Breakfast
©1989 David E. Kennedy

Page 42—An evening dinner at
Fredericksburg Herb Farm
©1995 Lynn A. Herrmann

Page 45—Path to retail shop
and tea room
Photograph by Texas Highways

Page 49—Varney's Chemist
Laden with cross garden
©1989 David E. Kennedy

Page 55—Fredericksburg Herb
Olive Oil, finalist for
Outstanding Condiment 1993
N.A.S.F.T.

Page 61—Retail shop at Christmas
©1992 Al Rendon

Page 66—Hanging herbs in
retail shop
©1992 Al Rendon

Page 74—Retail shop at Christmas
©1992 Al Rendon

Page 76—Vanilla Bean with
Chocolate Mint Ice Cream
©1995 Lynn A. Herrmann

Page 89—A portion of our back
garden and clay pots ready to
be planted
Photograph by Texas Highways

Page 95—Lemon Verbena
Peach Ice Cream
©1995 Lynn A. Herrmann

Page 100—A view of the Star
Garden with our manufactur-
ing facility in the background
Photograph by Texas Highways

Page 108—Fredericksburg
Herbal Vinegars and Herb
Olive Oil, including our
award-winning Edible
Flowers Herb Vinegar, first
place N.A.S.F.T. 1991
Outstanding Condiment
©1995 Lynn A. Herrmann

Page 110—Overview of the
Star Garden
Photograph by Texas Highways

Page 111—Our son Roy and
our Chinese pug Roman,
backgrounded by Hoja Santa,
a wonderful Mexican herb
©1995 Lynn A. Herrmann

Page 129—Fredericksburg
Edible Flower Preserves and
Herbal Pepper Preserves
©1995 Lynn A. Herrmann

Page 131—Edible Flower Salad
with Herbs de Provence
Vinaigrette, Fredericksburg
Herb Lemonade, and
French bread with Petal
Honey Butter
©1995 Lynn A. Herrmann

Page 135—A sampling of
Fredericksburg toiletries in
our glass etched bottles
©1995 Lynn A. Herrmann

Page 140—A typical herbal
lunch at Fredericksburg
Herb Farm
©1995 Lynn A. Herrmann

Page 149—Garden fountain,
surrounded by Bill's
potted herbs, at our first
store location

Page 163—Lemon Balm Bars
and Fredericksburg Herb
Lemonade on the patio of
the Herb Haus Bed and
Breakfast
©1995 Lynn A. Herrmann

Page 166—Fresh Peppermint
Fudge Brownies
©1989 Nell Simes

Back cover—Bill and Sylvia
Varney in the Star Garden at
the Herb Farm
©1995 Lynn A. Herrmann

Handmade papers
Langdell Papers
(802) 644-6647

Herb chart illustrated by
Lee Ethel
Hand lettering by
Sylvia Varney

Endpaper illustration
Yoli Rosenberg
(210) 257-2595